Lessons from the Trenches:

A Woman's Guide to Winning the Corporate Game

Erin Wolf

ISBN: 1-4392-2815-9

ISBN-13: 9781439228159

Visit www.booksurge.com to order additional copies.

Dedicated to Averil and Pierce

who are already working to make

the business world a better place

PREFACE

"The road to success is difficult because it is often disguised as hard work." – Anonymous

I started playing tennis when I was thirteen years old because the summer tennis pro at my family's club was living in our attic; his temporary housing had fallen through and we were his last resort. When I was fourteen, I played in my first tournament and reached the quarterfinals before losing to the first seed. At the end of that year, in love with the game, I vowed that I would attain a national ranking before turning sixteen. The skeptics said I had started the sport way too late in life to reach such lofty heights.

I didn't listen to them. Instead, I went over to my pro's house (he no longer lived in our attic) and had a serious discussion with him about my fledgling tennis career—or as serious a discussion as a 14-year-old can have about her life plans. After a lot of hard work, I qualified for national tournaments and received my first national ranking on target with my timeline. Later, at Duke University, a Division I school, I received one of the first and few athletic scholarships doled out to women in the late 1970s, played #2 singles on the varsity tennis team for four years, and never looked back.

During this time of seemingly easy achievement, I didn't think about discrimination or glass ceilings. I had attended an all-girls school for 14 years of my life—pre-K through 12th-grade—and therefore grew up in an environment where girls were the presidents, student council leaders, and sports team captains. In assuming leadership, the girls never had to work overtime to get people's attention. We never had to compete with boys for airtime in class nor did we receive less consideration because the teacher had his or her hands full with the rowdier guys. If anyone was acting up, it was always one of the girls.

My perception that the playing field was level for both men and women didn't change as I waltzed through Duke and Harvard Business School and secured my first jobs at IBM and on Wall Street. I believed I was in control of my destiny and that hard work would provide results. After all, I had been accepted by all the colleges to which I'd applied, landed a high-paying job out of college, and then graduated from one of the most prestigious business schools in the world. Following Harvard, I received offers from the cream of the consulting firms and investment banks. I was on my way.

It wasn't until much later that I realized I actually had experienced overt and covert forms of discrimination in the early years of my life. The first that I remember, subtle but relevant and informative, occurred in 1976—my first year at Duke— at the end of the varsity tennis season. I had maintained an outstanding won/lost record and was the only Duke player, male or female, to go undefeated that season in singles play. My doubles partner won the North Carolina Collegiate year-end tournament, and I was runner-up. This was a significant accomplishment for a first-year student given that there were many nationally ranked players attending North Carolina's colleges and universities and all were thrown into the same draw.

Because of our performance, my partner and I both qualified for the AIAW (then the equivalent of the NCAA for women) national tournament in June in Salt Lake City. As we began making plans to travel to Utah to represent Duke, I was suddenly informed that my school would not pay my way. Even though two of us had qualified, they would fund only one woman's travel expenses. This in spite of the fact that none of the men had qualified. Common sense says the school had budgeted to send at least one of the men to the national tournament had the men qualified. They couldn't say they didn't have the funds, but they did.

The second incident of a double standard that I remember was just as under the radar and just as troubling. When I was a junior or senior, the women's tennis team was doing very well and we received a lot of press in the school newspaper. After one particularly spectacular win that landed us on the front page of not only the school but also the Durham papers, my boyfriend, who had tried and failed to qualify for the varsity golf team, became moody.

When I finally got him to talk about it, he admitted that it was very difficult for him have a girlfriend who played a varsity sport—especially one who did it well. In his frame of reference, that situation was not the norm. I can only assume it would have been preferable for me to be a cheerleader, not a celebrated athlete.

As I look back, I can't help notice the irony in this turn of events. Most of the women on campus were standing in line to date any kind of varsity athlete and wore it like a badge of honor when they did. So why were all the girls proud of their varsity athlete boyfriends but not the reverse? Why was it a social stigma for a male to be dating a female athlete?

These different forms of discrimination did not end when I graduated from college but actually intensified. As I reflect upon incidents in the workplace, I am not altogether comfortable with what I see. I now realize that I *have* experienced many of the inequalities about which women complain.

Thinking about the positions that I've held in the rarified air of the executive suite, I've realized that life wasn't as easy as I had led myself to believe. I've frequently been excluded from important events—for no discernable reason. More than once I have not been invited to participate in company-sponsored golf outings, even though many of my male colleagues have a much higher handicap.

At one firm, when I was hired as the only female partner, I was told to sit in a cubicle even though the other two male partners occupied offices—and a third office was available. The next day, I brought in pictures of my children, plunked them down in that vacant office, and took a seat. Nobody said a thing. Had I not done that, however, I might have been relegated to that cubicle for the rest of my tenure.

Perhaps more importantly, I have been in positions where I was given less access to work referred in the office, to existing clients and to large-scale proposals, all of which affected my personal income.

I am looking at the workplace differently now because I have a 21-year-old daughter about to graduate from college and tackle the world. I don't want her to have to put up with some of the treatment I had to endure. Times have changed, but not enough. I have studied statistics that measure the achievements of women in business and have found some of them disturbing. I want to help pave the way for my daughter and women like her, but how?

I am not a journalist as Betty Friedan and Gloria Steinem were, and I have not won the Pulitzer Prize like Susan Faludi. I have, however, competed in top-level sports and worked for the best firms in the most competitive industries in the country. I have sat at the table with men and stayed there because I learned how to play the game—sometimes painfully—one rule at a time.

This book is dedicated to my daughter, Averil, and every other woman forging her way through the business world. I have a couple of pieces of advice for you: The first is to realize that you alone are in control of your future, so set your goals high and reach for them. If you can dream it, you can achieve it. The second is to understand that you don't have to reinvent the wheel. There are lessons to be learned from me and a host of other people. Decide which ones make sense to you and follow them. I hope this book will start you on your personal path to success.

SECTION I:
The Playing Field

Chapter One:
THE OTHER SIDE
OF REALITY

"Humankind cannot stand very much reality." – T.S. Eliot

"I believe in women!" These words captivated me when I heard them in a speech given by Johnetta Cole, former president of Spelman College. Looking at her towering figure on the podium, I nodded in agreement. I believed with all my heart that women could compete on any level or at least hold their own given an equal playing field.

A short time later, I came across an issue of *U.S. News & World Report* with a cover shot of three women. The title of the accompanying article written by Marci McDonald was, "Meet the New Generation of American CEOs: They're Young, Wired, Fearless—and Female." I remember feeling excited about this brave new world and the fact that women were finally making it to the top. I was captivated by the progress made by female professionals such as Carly Fiorina, who held a highly visible job as CEO of Hewlett-Packard, but also by women such as Lisa Henderson, one of the "fearless females," who had the audacity to go out on her own in the high-stakes world of entrepreneurship.

According to Henderson, she grew up poor but with a love of sports. She was awarded a scholarship to Missouri's Lindenwood University because she had a lot of talent and more than a little bit of luck. While watching a college soccer game as a high school senior, Henderson filled in for an absent player, proceeded to score two goals, and landed herself an athletic scholarship for the following year.

After graduation she worked for six years in marketing at Ralston Purina but was restless there because she had an entrepreneurial spirit and wanted to make a difference. With her background in sports and a desire to offer other young athletes an opportunity they might not otherwise have, Henderson turned her efforts to starting a company. She knew that high school students who played team sports could typically win college scholarships—if they knew where to look and especially if they came from well-known high schools. For players without big names or from smaller towns, those were and still are big "ifs." After Henderson brainstormed her ideas with colleagues and trusted advisors, she took the leap. Her vision was to create a database that would even the odds for college recruiting by tracking the performance of America's 10 million high school athletes.

In 2000, she launched LevelEdge.com. Within one week, 3,000 coaches signed up and investors including Goldman

Sachs and tennis star Billie Jean King injected $4 million in first-round financing into the venture. Henderson and her fellow female CEOs were pioneering into new areas for women.

This was a radically different environment from the one I faced when I graduated from Harvard Business School in 1984 and began interviewing for jobs. During the entire process, I was surrounded by men, both interviewers and interviewees. In fact, I don't remember encountering even one other woman. Most of the investment banks had no female partners and none of us interviewees, men or women, thought that was odd. When I accepted an offer from Salomon Brothers, my training class again consisted mainly of men.

Times have changed. The gains made by women in U.S. business during the past 40 years are unprecedented. Women experience freedom, independence, and opportunity about which our forebears could only dream.

According to the National Bureau of Labor Statistics, women currently comprise 48 percent of the U.S. labor force and 50 percent of the professional workforce. We are earning degrees from the best universities and landing top-echelon jobs. The contrasts between women in the 1960s and the present day are impossible to ignore. We have come from June Cleaver to *Sex and the City*, and from Betty Friedan and Gloria Steinem to Hilary Clinton and Meg Whitman. Our children have grown up with the knowledge that most mothers work outside the home just as most fathers do. Their doctors, dentists, and orthodontists may be male or female. A brother is as likely to be dragged along to his sister's softball game as she is to his Little League practice. Today, boys and girls assume they will have an equal opportunity to participate in important careers when they grow up.

These changes did not happen overnight. Many of women's advances have been the result of small inroads made during the last forty years. The constant progression of women into the workforce over time has resulted in an accompanying positive change in the type of work and level of positions we have achieved.

The percentage of the U.S. labor force occupied by women has grown slightly but steadily over the past four decades—from 38 percent in 1970 to a projected 48 percent in 2008, according to the U.S. Bureau of Labor Statistics.

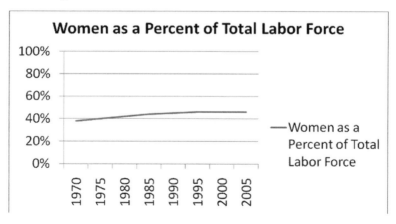

Source: Bureau of Labor Statistics

Our biggest advances have occurred since the early 1970s. From 1960-1975, the percent of women employed outside the home did indeed grow—from 37.7 percent in 1960 to 46.3% in 1975—but "housewife" was still the number one occupation for women. After 1975 and the passage of Title IX, the situation began to change. From 1975-1985, women posted gains in labor force participation, but more importantly they began to move into nontraditional jobs. By 1980, "housewife" had fallen to number eight of the top ten positions held by women, and by 1985 it had disappeared completely.

In the 21st century, there is no question that women have earned credibility in the business world. We are edging our way toward being 50 percent of the workforce and our opportunity landscape is changing dramatically. We are not just single career women, empty-nesters, or mothers working part-time for extra cash anymore.

As of 2005, 76.9 percent of working women were mothers with children age 6-17 according to the Bureau of Labor Statistics. Women are more educated and have more business experience than ever before, both of which have helped us attain higher-paying, more prestigious jobs. We are no longer trespassers on a man's turf but have cemented our inclusion in non-traditional roles for females by joining the ranks of CEOs, financial planners, engineers, astronauts, and computer analysts. We are nearly half of all middle management positions within the public sector. In this new millennium, women's accomplishments in the workplace are cause for unbridled celebration.

Or not. If we look at the stark facts, the reality is that we've come a long way—maybe. Females who attended business school in the 1980's are now experienced enough to garner positions of influence such as coveted board seats and corporate officer titles. However, actually attaining these high-power positions has proved elusive for most of us. Those "fearless" women who were on the cover of *Fortune* back in 2000 were the exception then just as they are today. They have found it difficult to compete even in today's "evolved" business environment. Carly Fiorina had a well-publicized exit from Hewlett-Packard even though hindsight proved her decisions during her CEO tenure to be sound. Lisa Henderson has chosen to stay in the world of small business post-LevelEdge but has not continued the level of visibility and influence that might have been expected by readers of McDonald's article on female leadership.

Women are well-represented in the lower and middle management ranks but woefully scarce in top-level positions. We are a minority based not on absolute numbers but rather on relative power and influence. Recent studies conducted by Catalyst, a research and advisory organization that works to advance women in business, confirm that women's accumulation of relevant experience has not translated into a proportional claim on leadership positions.

While the presence of female corporate officers within the Fortune 500 has been growing consistently over the past ten years, the numbers remain low. According to Catalyst, in 2007, 15.4 percent of corporate officers were women, compared to 8.7 percent in 1995. It's an improvement, but far short of what we can accomplish.

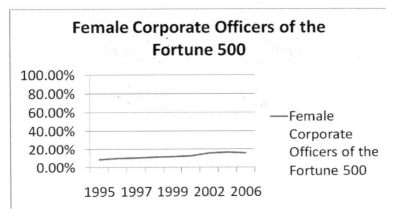

Female Corporate Officers of the Fortune 500

——Female Corporate Officers of the Fortune 500

1995 1997 1999 2002 2006

Source: Catalyst, Inc

Catalyst further reports that other titles within the Fortune 500 such as "top earner" and "senior executive" remain similarly elusive. In 1999, women held only 3.3 percent of top-earner spots (comprising the five most highly compensated positions) in Fortune 500 companies. As of 2007, we had improved our status to only 6.7 percent.

We do not fare well at securing the most elite positions of all: board members and chief executive officers. Fortune 500 board seats are the dominant and most desirable positions in U.S. business because these boards govern the country's largest companies. Unfortunately, women occupy a small percentage of U.S. boardrooms. In 1999, women held 685 or 11.2 percent of these coveted seats. By 2007, that number had grown to only 14.8 percent. Finally, it is hardly surprising that, in 2008, only 2.4 percent of CEOs in our country's largest 500 companies were female.

Although women have made many advances, it is a fact that, in business, men still wield the most power. On almost all measures of control, women come up short compared to our male counterparts. Whether it's the President's cabinet, the United States Congress, U.S. business, or American universities, men usually make the final decisions regarding policy, budget allocation, hiring, firing, promotion, and pay.

Since most human beings are most comfortable with those who look and act as they do, influential men typically will favor other males in these career-changing decisions *even if they do it subconsciously.* The fact that men are more comfortable working with other men—especially at the senior level—impedes the advancement of women.

Until women attain more positions of power in the workplace, the glass ceiling, though cracked, will remain intact. We need more women in high-level management roles so that we too will have the clout to influence decisions that in the past have been made by—and favor—men.

As more women move into the premier positions of U.S. business, government and education, both men and women will come to accept female leadership more easily. As long as men continue to hold the positions of power, the executive suite will be populated mainly by men. To earn our spot on the team, women must consistently demonstrate that we are just as smart, capable, fair, and *knowledgeable about what it takes to win.* We're making progress but still have much to accomplish.

Chapter Two:
STEREOTYPES, PERCEPTION AND PRIVILEGE: WHAT DO WOMEN REALLY WANT?

"Remember no one can make you feel inferior without your consent." – Eleanor Roosevelt

- "Women don't want to serve in leadership roles."
- "Women don't have what it takes."
- "Women are not strong enough to be good executives."

These myths are pervasive in business. Unfortunately, both men and women have heard them so often and for so long that we sometimes forget that they're not true. Independent studies demonstrate a far different reality.

Fiction: Women are not as committed to their careers as men.

Fact: A 2001 Korn Ferry survey reported that only one-third of female respondents had ever taken a leave of absence. Not including maternity leave, more men took leaves than women.

Fiction: Women will not work long hours.

Fact: The same survey showed that women worked the same number of hours as their male counterparts.

Fiction: Women cannot or will not relocate.

Fact: Only 14.1 percent of the women surveyed refused relocation versus 20 percent of men.

Fiction: Women are more nurturing than men.

Fact: In the Korn Ferry survey, "concern for people" was cited as important by 33 percent of men, but only 18 percent of women.

Fiction: Women lack quantitative skills.

Fact: Numerous studies have shown that the distribution of men and women in mathematical ability is only .15 standard deviations apart.

The harsh reality is that women have to overcome a whole constellation of negative perceptions in the workplace. Although both sexes have equal desires to be CEOs and pursue similar strategies for advancing in—or leaving—a company, women face environmental challenges, inequalities, and discrimination that make their pursuit of success more difficult than that of men.

Myths about women's abilities and performance are persistent perhaps because they serve men's purposes. They arise from stereotypes, misperceptions, and the role of privilege.

Stereotyping and Privilege

Gender stereotypes are socially shared beliefs regarding characteristics or attributes that define men and women *in general* and influence our perceptions of men and women *as individuals*. Stereotypes tend to exaggerate the perceived differences *between* groups and the perceived similarities *within* groups. The problem with stereotypes is that they usually lead us to judge people based on incorrect information, biases, or outdated ideas; they usually do more harm than good.

It seems as if men and women are stereotyped from birth. Baby girls wear pink, while boys wear blue. Girls are made of "sugar, spice and everything nice," but boys aren't. A friend of mine has 4-year-old twins (boy and girl) who provide a veritable petri dish for studying how we put our children into predetermined gender boxes from a very early age. I looked with amazement at the party invitation sent out for the twins' most recent birthday: the girls were told to dress as cheerleaders and the boys as football players, firmly establishing who was on the front line and who was in a supporting role.

In their book *Women and Men in Organizations*, Jeanette Cleveland, Margaret Stockdale, and Kevin Murphy report on non-biased surveys given to both men and women over several years. They discovered that the following adjectives are often used to describe the two sexes:

Male Traits	Female Traits
Intellectually rational	Emotional
Realistic	Affectionate
Tough	Flirtatious
Aggressive	Warm
Dominant	Attractive
Assertive	Nurturing
Strong	Understanding
Powerful	Dependent
Decisive	Empathetic

It is not surprising that the adjectives attributed to men are those we associate most with success in business. Those that are assigned to women are not. Gender stereotypes convey the idea that men should have power or influence over women particularly when acting in what traditionally has been man's domain—the workplace. Female stereotypes are still relatively negative and annoyingly based on the cumulative perception that business is not a normal environment for us.

What's worse is many researchers contend that stereotyping increases for the underrepresented group in a given situation (in the workplace, that's women) and as a result of the underrepresentation, stereotyping is exaggerated. The visibility of "typical" female behavior in business is spotlighted and therefore more closely scrutinized. We often hear women complain that they can't get away with the same behavior men exhibit, and the truth is they can't. The same behavior is interpreted and treated differently.

For example, if a woman is emotional in a staff meeting, people will notice *and remember,* while a man's emotions are often silently written off. If a man yells in a meeting, people sit up and listen; if a woman yells, she is perceived as bitchy and unreasonable. While many women are frustrated with the stereotypes that cling to us like lint, our male counterparts often welcome the stereotypes applied to them because those stereotypes usually work to a man's advantage.

Unfortunately, stereotyping can lead to harmful discrimination against women in business. One of the most famous—and litigated—cases involving stereotyping and discrimination was brought 25 years ago by a woman named Ann Hopkins. In 1982, Price Waterhouse, one of the then Big Eight accounting firms, had 662 partners, seven of whom were women. That year, Hopkins, a senior manager who had been with the firm for five years, was proposed for partnership along with 87 men.

In a statement supporting her candidacy, the partners in Hopkins' office highlighted her successful two-year effort to secure $25 million worth of business. Her performance was labeled "outstanding" and her work was described as "virtually at the partner level." None of the other male candidates had a comparable record in terms of successfully securing major contracts for the firm.

Furthermore, according to court documents, partners in her office praised her character describing her as an "outstanding professional" who had a "deft touch," a "strong character, independence, and integrity." Her clients viewed her as "extremely competent, intelligent," "strong and forthright, very productive, energetic, and creative." She was also considered a "stimulating conversationalist." With all of these positive attributes, as well as her success in selling work, one would have thought that Hopkins would be a shoo-in for partner.

However, of the 88 people proposed for partnership that year, 20—including Hopkins—were "held" for reconsideration the following year. When the partners in her office refused to propose her again the next year, she sued the partnership under Title VII of the Civil Rights Act, charging that the firm had discriminated against her on the basis of sex. She charged that "sex stereotyping" played a role in the evaluation of her as a partner candidate. The courts agreed with her.

There were clear signs that some of the partners reacted negatively to Hopkins's personality because she did not demonstrate the behavior expected of a woman. One partner described her as "macho," while another objected to her use of profanity even though off-color language was rampant among the men. The reason the firm gave her for not qualifying as partner material was that she was too abrasive, especially to staff members, even though this behavior from the male partners was typical.

Adding insult to injury, the partner who was responsible for explaining the reasons for the board's decision told

Hopkins that she could improve her chances for partnership if she would "walk more femininely, talk more femininely, dress more femininely, wear make-up, have her hair styled, and wear jewelry."

Although the Price Waterhouse partners could have emphasized interpersonal skills in partnership decisions, their attitudes toward Hopkins instead reflected sex stereotyping. Instead of emphasizing what was unacceptable for *any* partner candidate, they implied from their statements that Hopkins's level of aggressiveness was unacceptable only for a *female* partner candidate.

It is exasperating that Hopkins was censured for demonstrating the very characteristics that reward men so generously in the workplace. Since the early 1970s, researchers have repeatedly shown that many traits associated with management and leadership are seen as male traits and that stereotypes of "leader" seem to overlap substantially with the male stereotype. Therefore, many businesswomen find themselves in a double bind. If they act like men, they are too aggressive. If they act like women, they don't have what it takes.

Stereotypes lead to inequalities (and, as in Hopkins' case, outright discrimination) in the workplace by indicating greater perceived differences between the sexes than actually exist. For example, although there are few real differences in speech used by both men and women, there is much evidence of perceived difference. The male communication style pegs men as dominant and authoritative—both traits that translate to management material.

Many men also perceive that women want something different from their careers than men do. I have experienced more than one male executive's worrying about hiring highly qualified female employees because they are afraid that the women will eventually have children and drop out of the workforce. These employers believe that hiring males is safer.

I also have worked at a firm where female vice presidents were allowed to work part-time for family reasons, but males were not. While this may seem very open-minded and 21st century, I believe it to be discriminatory and patronizing to both the men and women involved. If women can work part-time for family reasons, men should be able to as well. A male friend of mine who has primary responsibility for his son was incensed by this double standard. He petitioned the office lead for equal rights for men, citing that the company was promoting a double standard. He was correct. Our goal should be to have employers treat women equally in all respects. Women should not be singled out as special-needs employees.

Most women complain about and want to dispel sex-based stereotyping because it hurts us on the job. Unfortunately, we usually feel powerless to do so and men typically do not help with this issue. In most social organizations, the privileged or dominant groups, whether male or female, try to preserve or expand the advantages that their group enjoys even if they do it subconsciously. In the workplace, men benefit from the fact that the playing field is not level—and most men don't want to give that up.

Preservation of Dominance

Men can maintain and even increase their dominance in the workplace through a variety of tactics. One is by maintaining power over recruitment and promotion decisions. Currently, men have far more influence in these decisions, especially at senior levels. Research cited by Cleveland, Stockdale, and Murphy, has shown that men are more likely to be hired for professional and managerial positions than similarly qualified women. Women are also less likely to be promoted or are promoted at a slower rate than men. In fact, even when women receive higher performance ratings than men, men receive more promotions. There is continued evidence that in business, government, and professional occupations, the proportion of women decreases as the rank or status of the position increases.

Unfortunately, I have experienced the preservation of dominance and the "fewer women at the top than at the bottom" syndrome more than once. One example occurred at a large, professional services firm where I was one of four female partners, representing a whopping 10 percent of the partnership. Of the five levels within the firm, women represented only 10 percent of the top two but—surprise!—50 percent of the entry level. When asked why there were so few women at the top nationwide, one daring and honest male colleague stated that the current partners were more comfortable hiring managing directors with whom they had previously worked. Of course, those were other males.

In fact, in my office, the managing partner boasted that to be considered for employment, you had to have previously worked with someone within the firm. I often wondered why I, an outsider, had been hired. I later realized that it was solely for my connections; I clearly was not part of the inner circle. Our office was made up of a group of men who had followed each other from company to company. Those with the power and influence to bring in top-level executives were hiring those with whom they were most comfortable—white males–and perpetuating the privilege. This did not make them bad people. It did, however, make them poor leaders because their approach did not afford them the opportunity to hire the most qualified men or women for the jobs.

The irony of all of this is that companies with greater gender diversity in the executive suite outperform those with fewer women. In their Harvard Business Review article "Managing Diversity," David Thomas, an associate professor at Harvard Business School, and Robin Ely, an associate professor at Columbia Business School, contend that until recently companies felt they should concern themselves with diversity because discrimination is both morally and legally wrong. Thomas and Ely further assert that today's managers believe that a more diverse workforce will increase organizational effectiveness as it will "lift morale, bring greater access to new segments of the marketplace, and enhance productivity." In other words, diversity will be good for business.

Indeed, recent McKinsey & Company research shows that companies with higher numbers of women at senior levels perform better both financially and organizationally than companies with less diversity. In addition, work by professors at

Columbia and University of Maryland business schools, using data on 1,500 U.S companies, demonstrates a "strong positive association between return on assets, return on equity and the [female top management] participation rate."

Thomas and Ely state that the reason diversity helps the bottom line has nothing to do with fairness or access to new markets or morale lifting. They contend that groups outside of the white male mainstream bring more that just insider information. They bring "different, important, and competitively relevant knowledge and perspectives about how to actually *do work*—how to design processes, reach goals, frame tasks, create effective teams, communicate ideas, and lead. When allowed to, members of these groups can help companies grow and improve by challenging basic assumptions about an organization's functions, strategies, operations, practices, and procedures." Thomas and Ely, McKinsey, and others have proven that men who continue to perpetuate "men on top" are actually doing their organizations a disservice.

Unfortunately, sexism remains the last widely unchallenged form of discrimination in this country. We have made great strides in understanding that discrimination based on race, religion, or nationality is wrong, but we haven't quite gotten there with sex. There are still golf clubs women can't join, and it is still okay to call poor-performing male athletes "ladies." More than once, I have been in a foursome consisting of three men and me during which one of the men calls another "Alice" (or "Sue" or "Sarah") after his male compatriot misses a putt. This behavior is humiliating because it is using the sex to which

I belong as a slur. I feel as if I am the recipient of their bigotry despite the fact that this member of the "weaker sex" is the one walking the course and carrying her own bag while they ride in a cart—and I often have a better score.

Discrimination based on race or religion is now taboo. In today's society, it is generally considered unacceptable to make racial and religious slurs and most of us are shocked when this occurs. Yet the same shock and embarrassment does not occur within the population at large when women are the brunt of derisive jokes and comments. This mindset is alive and well in business.

Most women have experienced inequalities in the workplace. We have labored under perceptions that are unfair and untrue and put up with treatment that other minorities fought to eliminate long ago. But we have not stopped trying to make the workplace better for ourselves and for the next generation. Most of us believe that it is our job to stop the stereotyping, myths and negative perceptions that follow us around like an unwanted suitor. We also know that we have a much better chance of influencing these changes when we reach positions of power. Our goal is to figure out how to reach these coveted roles. The advice in the following chapters is meant to position you at the start of the race and propel you through to the finish line by teaching you the rules of the game and the tactics needed to win. The rest is up to you.

Chapter Three
DEGREES OF SUCCESS: WOMEN AND EDUCATION

"Only the educated are free." – Epictetus

It was not long ago that our society was not as focused on educating our women as we were our men. Because women were not expected to pursue serious careers, we were not afforded the same access to higher education as our male counterparts. An October 16, 1956, *Look* magazine editorial sums up the prevailing opinion of our role in the workplace should be:

The American woman is winning the battle of the sexes. Like a teenager, she is growing up and confounding her critics. ... No longer a psychological immigrant to man's world, she works, rather casually, as a third of the U.S. labor force, less towards a 'big career' than as a way of filling a hope chest or buying a new home freezer. She gracefully concedes the top jobs to men. This wondrous creature also marries younger than ever, bears more babies and looks and acts far more feminine than the 'emancipated' girl of the 1920s or even '30s. Steelworker's wife and Junior Leaguer alike do their own housework. ... Today, if she makes an old-fashioned choice and lovingly tends a garden and a bumper crop of children, she rates higher hosannas than ever before.

As late as the 1960s, guidance counselors in schools across the country advised girls against taking difficult subjects, explaining that they were a waste of time. "Mate Selection," "Adjustment to Marriage," and "Education for Family Living" were included as course offerings at a prominent women's college. The school's slogan was, "We are not educating women to be scholars; we are educating them to be wives and mothers."

In the 1950s, many elite boarding schools for girls were simply finishing schools that prepared their students for marriage rather than for higher education. Even in the 1960s, some schools that now are considered important feeders to Ivy League colleges offered girls two educational tracks: finishing school or college prep. Most girls didn't think to question the fact that only one track was offered at boys' schools.

Prior to the 1970s, colleges and universities themselves made it more difficult for women to access higher education. Many institutions required women to have higher test scores and better grades than male applicants to gain admission. Sometimes the discrimination was overt: At the University of

Virginia, women could enroll in the School of Education or the School of Nursing, but Virginia state law prohibited them from being admitted to the College of Arts and Sciences. It was only by court order in 1970 that the first woman was allowed to study something other than education or nursing at UVA. Sometimes the discrimination was more subtle. The University of North Carolina, for example, limited the number of women students by requiring them to live on campus where there was insufficient housing. At some schools, particular classes were off-limits to women. Female students often were excluded from enrolling in higher-level math or science courses to ensure space for male students. We were indeed the unwelcome stepchildren of academia.

Many private colleges and universities were also all-male until the 1970s and some finally admitted women grudgingly. According to a former board member of an Ivy League school, the debate about whether or not to accept women revolved around annual giving. The school was worried that its endowment would suffer if women were among its graduates. They surmised that men earned the money and controlled the finances in most households and therefore gave to the institutions they deemed worthy. Women didn't wield the same clout.

Donna Manning, former Executive Director at Catalyst, painfully recalls how things used to be prior to the 1970s. A good math student, Donna was enrolled in a public high school in Southern California. One semester, as she went to sign up for a trigonometry course that was not yet filled, she was told that she couldn't take it because the open spaces were reserved for the male students. Her faculty advisor appealed to the math department to no avail. Donna could not take any legal action as there were no laws in place to support her. Nowadays, it is difficult to imagine how this could ever have happened.

Another victim of educational bias against women was Leslie Christian, a vice president at Salomon Brothers in the 1980s. Leslie is a woman who succeeded despite the fact that both our educational system and society worked against her. A high school student in the 1960s, Leslie was brilliant with numbers and had close to an 800 on her math SAT without the benefit of the hours of coaching many students get nowadays. As she tells it, "Back then we didn't even think of preparing for the test. We just went in and took it." One would have thought that a college or career counselor would have encouraged Leslie to exploit her talent for numbers. She could have considered any number of schools to enhance her quantitative skills; she could have pursued engineering or high-level math.

Instead, she was counseled to major in English at the University of Washington because "that's what young women did" and subsequently accepted a position teaching high school grammar. Although Leslie was a good English teacher, she finally realized that she was not using her real talents. In the 1970s, she decided to enter the world of finance, where she could put her analytical skills to good use. She rose quickly within the organization because finally she was where she belonged. It's unfortunate that it took her longer than necessary to get there.

The passage of Title IX in 1972 changed everything. Women's second-class status in education was upgraded almost overnight. And you thought Title IX was all about sports? The legislation was actually enacted for academic purposes; sports were a bonus. The law is clear: Title IX of the Education Amendments of 1972 prohibits discrimination on the basis of sex in educational programs and activities at educational institutions that receive federal funds. It affects all curricular and extracurricular offerings from medicine, law, and science to drama, dance, and athletics.

The origin of Title IX lies in the 1965 presidential Executive Order 11246 prohibiting federal contractors from discrimination in employment on the basis of race, color, religion, or national origin. Executive Order 11246 was amended by President Johnson, effective October 13, 1968, to include discrimination based on sex.

Bernice R. Sandler, at the time a part-time lecturer at the University of Maryland, was the first person to use the order for the benefit of women. "I had made the connection," she said, "that, since most universities and colleges had federal contracts, they were forbidden from discriminating in employment on the basis of sex." Encouraged by Sandler's efforts, on March 9, 1970, Rep. Martha Griffiths (D-Michigan) spoke to the U.S. Congress concerning discrimination against women in education. Three weeks later, the first contract compliance investigation involving sex discrimination began at Harvard University.

In June and July 1970, Rep. Edith Green (D-Ohio), who chaired the subcommittee that dealt with higher education, drafted legislation prohibiting sex discrimination in education and held the first congressional hearings on the education and employment of women. The hearings were the first legislative step toward the enactment of Title IX.

Since this legislation was passed, our academic accomplishments have been nothing short of spectacular. Over the last 30 years, nearly all of the progress in educational attainment has been achieved by females. For example, in 1969, 42 percent of BAs conferred by degree-granting institutions were awarded to women. By 2005, that proportion had jumped to 57 percent according to the National Center for Education Statistics, and that percentage has held steady. Women are graduating from prestigious institutions with impressive degrees—all of which is important to our being accepted in the workplace.

Percentage of BA Degrees Conferred by Sex

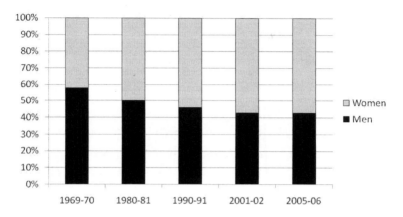

Source: National Center for Educational Statistics

Typically, math and science have been labeled as male courses. Most businesses, which in the past were hiring mainly men, expected or required a certain number of these analytical courses to be listed on an applicant's transcript. Being denied admission to these classes put women at a clear disadvantage from a business perspective. Because Title IX opened up access for females to all subjects in school, we have seen a dramatic shift in the number of women taking classes in, majoring in, and working in advanced math and science fields.

Female participation in high school math classes alone paled in comparison to that of men before the passage of Title IX. By 1994 the percentages of women taking algebra, geometry, and calculus in high school—68 percent, 70 percent, and nine percent respectively–were similar to the percentages of males taking those courses. Due to more opportunities for girls to take math and science classes in high school, many more college women are majoring in these and other traditionally male subjects. According to the National Council of Educational Statistics, in 1962, only 27 percent of undergraduate degrees in math were awarded to women. By 2005, that number had increased to 46 percent.

The increase in female engineering graduates from The Georgia Institute of Technology tells the story of our progress, one year at a time. Though Georgia Tech currently awards more undergraduate engineering degrees to women than any other engineering school according to the American Society for Engineering Education, in the 1920s, the Board of Regents voted to ban women from attending the school. In the early 1950s, the president of Georgia Tech had a daughter who wanted to enroll in the college but she was forced to go elsewhere because old 1920s rules were still in place.

By 1952, the Board of Regents voted to allow women back into the school—it was a very close vote. For the next twenty years, the number of women attaining engineering degrees remained low. In 1970, only five of the 765 students graduating with an engineering degree were female. By 1979, after the passage of Title IX, 139 of the 890 engineering graduates were women—certainly an improvement. More recently, in 2008, 282 of the 1177 engineering degrees were awarded to women. The landscape is still not perfect but it has improved. The perception that males have an innate edge in certain subjects while not gone is at least lessened.

The ability to take upper-level math and science courses paved the way for women such as Sally Ride, the first U.S. female astronaut, to catapult themselves into careers formerly open only to men. Ride's background is well-known. Born in 1951 in Encino, California, Ride's first significant accomplishments were in sports—she won a tennis scholarship to Westlake School for Girls in Los Angeles and upon graduation, entered Swarthmore College. She subsequently dropped out of school to pursue a professional tennis career. In an epiphany similar to mine, Ride realized that her athletic prowess wasn't sufficient for the competitive world of professional tennis. She returned to her education, enrolling at Stanford University. There, she quickly excelled.

In 1977, she was 27 years old with a bachelor of science in Physics, a bachelor of arts in English, a master of science in Physics, and was a Ph.D. candidate looking for postdoctoral work in astrophysics. She picked up the Stanford University newspaper, read about NASA's search for astronauts and decided to apply along with 8,000 others. Thirty-five were accepted to the program, including six women, one of whom was Sally Ride.

After receiving her acceptance as an astronaut in January, 1978, Ride began a one-year training and evaluation period. She learned parachute jumping, water survival, gravity and weightlessness training, radio communications, and navigation, passing with flying colors. In 1983, Ride became the first American woman in space as an astronaut on the shuttle Challenger.

While Ride's story may be atypical, numbers show that women's performance in the classroom has unquestionably contributed to our success in attaining higher numbers in the labor force and in securing better jobs. In and of itself, this is a reason for optimism. However, despite these educational gains, we are still not acquiring commensurate positions of power and influence. Is it coincidence, then, that the one academic statistic that sticks out like a sore thumb is our inability to achieve parity in graduate business school programs?

Harvard Business School provides a good example. "Complete integration" of females at Harvard's Graduate School of Business Administration took place when eight women were admitted to the Class of 1965. Years later, when I walked those hallowed halls in the mid-1980s, women accounted for about a quarter of my class. Today, the MBA class of 2009 "boasts" 324 women or 36 percent of those enrolled. How can Harvard Business School be boastful of a mere 36 percent when the ratio of men to women in law and medical schools has reached parity?

The number of women in top MBA programs has remained generally unchanged for more than a decade. In 1994, women on average made up only 28 percent of the top 20 MBA programs and by 2005 that number only increased to 29.7 percent. By not attaining top degrees in business at the same rate as men, we are certainly not helping our odds of climbing to the top rungs of the corporate ladder in the near future.

Why are more women attracted to law, medicine, and other graduate pursuits rather than business? One answer is that women embarking on their careers are not entirely comfortable with what they see once they leave the classroom. They are confronted with the image of Gordon Gekko in the 1987 movie *Wall Street*. Gekko, a financial bigwig, was motivated by only money. Most people remember the famous scene in which Gekko tells his impressionable young colleague to win at all costs and that "greed is good." This clearly isn't the world many of us choose to join.

We also don't like the fact that when we do choose to join the business world, most of us still find ourselves forced to eat at the kids' table in the kitchen while the big boys are in the dining room—or the boardroom. I learned long ago that career success requires more than smarts and ability. Perceptions about what skills are necessary to "make it" in business put educational achievement low on the list.

Gaining the requisite education is simply ground zero for us. The traits that really catapult a businessperson to success are not always those that we can absorb from a classroom. Characteristics such as charisma, risk-taking, and inspiring identification among followers are ascribed to many leaders but are very subjective qualities and difficult to measure. Is a little charisma enough? How much is too much? How do we inspire identification when most of those doing the identifying are white males?

To make matters more difficult, women often feel that they have to walk a behavioral tightrope. We must learn how to lead without seeming strident or too domineering, how to show enough emotion to seem passionate but not so much as to seem weak, how to support our direct reports without seeming too nurturing.

In business, we don't get ahead by using our education and knowledge to fix a broken leg or write a brilliant brief. We succeed when we play by the rules of a game that was created long ago by men and perfected by them over the years. For many women, entering the world of business is like taking a test without being given access to the textbook, stepping onto an athletic field without knowing the sport in which we're supposed to be participating, or playing a game without knowing the rules.

One way to change our reality is to understand what those at the top do differently and then use this newfound knowledge to our advantage.

Chapter Four:
THE LUCKY SEVEN

"It's better to be lucky than good" – Anonymous

In today's business environment, success is most often measured by the money you make or the power you wield. Although your own personal method of self-evaluation may be different, the world still equates success with the size of your paycheck or your position on the corporate ladder.

Since the purpose of a for-profit business is to make money for its shareholders, it stands to reason that those who help increase the bottom line should rise higher and earn more than those who don't. If it actually worked this way, the business environment would be a very objective meritocracy. But it doesn't.

Promotions, raises, and entry into the executive suite are based on many factors that are often difficult to quantify. Some people think the most important of these factors is education, but if academic credentials were the key to upward mobility, women would be running the world today. Since we're not, the key to success must be something else.

That something else is what most men know. They are familiar with the requirements for success in business because these requirements have been ingrained in them since childhood. Most boys *and their parents* don't question whether the males in the family will work for a living. Unless they are independently wealthy, most men don't consider other options. From the beginning of time, boys have been raised to provide for themselves at the very least and usually for a family and children as well. Most of the male existence is career focused. Often their very self-worth is intertwined with their ability to achieve more than their peers, especially in terms of accumulation of financial wealth and material possessions. For most men, the old expression that he who dies with the most toys wins is a sentiment that rings true. Men live and play in a business world that their forefathers created many years ago and perfected along the way.

Women, on the other hand, may have been raised to provide for themselves or not. Society gives its girls an option that it doesn't give its boys: to raise a family in lieu of pursuing a career. Most girls are therefore reared differently from boys. From the time they are young, sons are included in the age-old rituals designed by and for males. At the golf course across from my house, I see fathers out playing a few holes in the early evening with their young sons but rarely with their daughters. Until recently, boys' sports teams commanded much more attention than girls'. And when was the last time you heard of a father taking his daughter hunting? These rituals are part of the fundamental, non-academic training that is a prerequisite for understanding the games that are played in the workplace.

I was lucky enough to be part of one of these traditions when I was very young. My family lived in Cleveland in the 1960s and all the men followed professional football and were rabid Browns fans.

The executives in my father's office trudged to the games every Sunday with their sons in tow. Since there were two daughters and no sons in my family, I being the younger and more easily persuaded, accompanied my father and played the role of Number One son at these outings. We would sit in the stands in single digit temperatures and root for our favorite team.

I loved the opportunity not only to bond with my father without my pesky sister around but also to feel like one of the inner circle. From grade school on, I could talk the talk. I understood the difference between a field goal and an extra kick, between the offense and the defense. I knew which teams were in contention for the plays-offs and which were lame ducks.

With red cheeks and frozen fingers, my father, his friends, their sons, and I lamented another year of the Browns' not quite measuring up. This early indoctrination to a time-honored male-bonding ritual has caused me to feel more comfortable in the workplace when the talk turns to professional sports. Once I mention my childhood experience with the hapless Browns, I am instantly accepted.

Those who think the key to getting ahead is to do their jobs well and even to work above and beyond what is expected of them are missing the complete landscape of the business world.

A whole host of contests and competitions is being played around them. These games may have little impact on the company from a financial standpoint, but they improve the status of those who participate in them. Most men understand and know how to use this informal system. Most women do not. We don't understand the rules and we don't speak the language. The progress that we have made in gaining higher and better degrees has gotten us only so far.

What makes matters worse is that when it comes to workplace dynamics, many women have a tough time knowing what we know versus knowing what we don't know. A senior partner at Bain & Company used to explain this phenomenon succinctly to his colleagues:

- We are aware of what we know
- We are sometimes aware of what we don't know

BUT

- We are most often **unaware of what we don't know**

He depicted this reality on a pie chart that was brilliant in its simplicity:

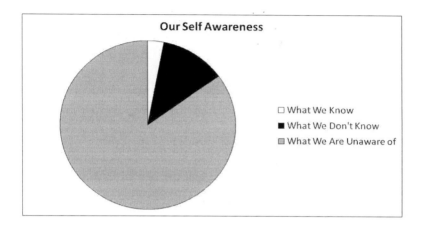

Women in business are often unaware of what we don't know, and this puts us at a disadvantage to men. We are unaware of the spoken and unspoken rules of the corporate games that are played out in executive suites and boardrooms across the country. We don't know the secret handshake or use the right words. We often don't understand that it takes more than hard work to make it to the top. We need to become aware of *what we don't know*, and then use this knowledge to advance ourselves.

The secret code of business is not that complex. However, it seems perplexing to many women because it is inspired by the male way of doing things. From the time they are young, males are expected to get the job done even if it means making a few enemies along the way. Females, however, are expected to make everybody happy. The stereotypical family includes a father who solves the problems and a mother who keeps the peace.

In business, men naturally expect workplace behavior to reflect the male reality. Men tend to use more sports analogies when discussing issues. They are usually more forthright in their speech and message delivery. They are not afraid of conflict. Their style is different from that of most women, and this difference creates confusion at work. Men don't understand why women aren't playing by the rules; women aren't even aware that there are rules.

I have seen exceptional women passed over for promotion because they did not didn't understand the politics of business. At one well-known firm, the difference in level of awareness of corporate politics by two junior consultants, Tom and Joan, was striking and resulted in dramatic consequences for their respective careers at the firm. Tom, thirty years old, had an undergraduate degree and a few years' work experience. Joan had an MBA from a top-25 school and more work experience than Tom.

However, the biggest difference between the two was not academic success or years on the job. The different was that Tom knew exactly how to work the system and curry favor with the person in the office with the most power to affect his future—the managing partner. Joan did not.

Tom quickly became the managing partner's "go to" guy. He was promoted faster than others. Joan did not understand the peripheral machinations of the office and did not play the game. She worked hard, assumed that the system would reward her exceptional performance—and was passed over for promotion that should have been a slam dunk. Tom, with less education, less work experience and fewer billable hours than Joan, became senior to Joan. Ability level had nothing to do with this discrepancy. Knowledge of how to play the game did.

For many years, I have tried to grab a seat in the business equivalent of musical chairs. As I have risen higher on the organizational chart, I have found it more difficult to find that seat. The competition for a place on the executive team or a partner title is intense and a zero-sum game. Few females garner these coveted positions or are even vying for them. Those who manage to reach them have cracked the code. They exhibit behaviors—their personal keys to success—that propel them to their lofty positions. While many women possess the requisite intelligence and other wonderful qualities to be successful, exceptional businesswomen and men possess something more, something that allows them to rise above the rest of the corporate crowd or makes their entrepreneurial ventures flourish.

These female leaders have developed their own playbooks for achievement. The glass ceiling-breakers exhibit characteristics that are similar to those of their male peers. These women aren't more "masculine" and don't try to be one of the guys. But they consistently follow certain rules that contribute to the achievement of their business goals, however far-reaching those goals may be.

I call these rules The Lucky Seven, and they aren't hard to understand:

1. Learn the plays that make up the game of business.
2. Help other women ... and men.
3. Apply for membership in the good old boy network. Today.
4. Brand your passion.
5. Own the illusion of confidence.
6. Reach beyond your comfort zone.
7. Remember it's not life or death. It's only business.

As you begin to apply these rules every day, you'll become more aware of what you don't know. You'll learn to understand the different plays being laid out by your coaches and teammates. And if more women truly come to know what goes on in the workplace, perhaps we can take a hammer to the glass that's been hanging over our heads for much too long.

SECTION II:
The Lucky Seven in Action

Chapter Five :
LUCK SEVEN RULE 1:
LEARN THE PLAYS THAT MAKE UP THE GAME OF BUSINESS

"Winning isn't everything; it's the only thing" – Vince Lombardi, *1970s*

"I wish to hell I'd never said that damn thing. ... I sure as hell didn't mean for people to crush human value and morality." – Vince Lombardi, *1990s*

It's March and the craziness is just beginning to set in. The draw has been posted, and everyone's sending and receiving e-mails with the latest office pool information. Rules of play have been set; employees are more intent on picking their favorite teams than checking their BlackBerries®. Nobody is talking about anything other than who is seeded, who will be the first upset (will a #16 seed ever beat a #1?), and when the next

Cinderella team will emerge. If any of this sounds familiar, you know I'm describing the NCAA men's basketball tournament, more commonly referred to as "March Madness."

This tournament epitomizes the close connection between sports and business. Those of us who have been in the workplace for more than a few years understand that the business environment mirrors all of the competition and objective measures of success, such as win-loss records, that most males lived for as young boys. Business is a constant re-creation of the Little League baseball and Pee-Wee football our male colleagues enjoyed in their formative years. Business is a game with its own set of rules and its own way of scoring.

Not only is business run as a game, but the participants also like or pretend to like sports. Workers can be accepted by understanding the rules of sports and their relationship to the rules of business.

I have been fortunate in understanding early on that business is a game, and I have generally tried to play by the rules. I have also benefited immensely from having been involved in high-level sports with men all my life. I've instinctively treated every working relationship and business transaction as if it were a game—and I knew the rules. I've always understood what the goal was (to win the game), what was expected of me (to contribute whatever I could so that we would win the game), how to get there (follow the bosses' instructions and be creative when necessary so we could win the game), and what the scoring system was (so I would know if/when I won). However, I know that I am the anomaly.

In addition to participating in sports, I also enjoy playing and watching sports of all flavors. I remember cheering when Monday Night Football was first introduced. Before that, we only had Sundays! I can rattle off professional baseball and college basketball stats with the best of them. This instantly puts men at ease. I am not from Venus; I am one of them.

Many women are at a loss in an ultra-competitive environment filled with macho posturing and game playing. We did not make up the rules and now feel as if we are being asked to compete without the benefit of a playbook. If you are in a work situation where game-playing is rampant and sports is a common theme among the men, I advise you to hone your sports knowledge so you are at least conversant with what the guys are talking about (see "Quick Tip" at the end of this chapter), and to learn the rules of the game of business. Those who talk the talk are more easily accepted. Those who know the rules and play by them succeed.

From years of observation and practice, I have identified several rules of engagement that have worked for me. To win, you must observe several simple rules. Here they are:

- *Be internally supportive, externally competitive*

When I was an undergraduate at Duke University, I competed on the varsity tennis team at the #2 singles position all four years and loved every minute of it. Unlike the days I played national junior tournaments as a sole participant, I was now part of a team. We supported each other, celebrated our victories and bemoaned our losses—and we didn't compete against one another. I never challenged the #1 player and the #3 did not challenge me. For two consecutive years, our #1, Cindy Johnson, was the winner of the North Carolina state collegiate tournament and I was the runner-up. We were exactly where we should be in the lineup and everyone knew it. While I might have beaten Cindy on any given day, I would not do so consistently. I belonged at the #2 position.

Our arch rivals, the women's tennis team of the University of North Carolina, had a very different philosophy. They challenged each other constantly. I never knew against whom I'd play when they arrived on our campus. Their team was built on internal competition.

What I learned from this situation was that internal support was better than internal competition. Our teams were ranked higher nationally, and year after year we were able to recruit top players. More importantly, I played better because of our culture. I focused more on beating our competitors than on protecting my internal turf. And that made all the difference.

Children who play team sports learn at an early age that a team must work well together in order to win. The whole should be better than the sum of its parts. If you have great individual players who don't work well together, you will probably lose to a team, even a less-talented team, that does. Sports teach athletes to promote team harmony, to support their teammates rather than criticize them, and to emphasize strengths rather than weaknesses. The group is more important than the individual.

Mike Krzyzewski, Duke University men's basketball coach, proves the importance of team loyalty and internal support. His players are regularly recognized as the most unselfish players in college sports. Instead of each going for the glory individually, they get the ball to the player who has the greatest chance of scoring. This strategy helped them win the NCAA championship in 1992.

That year, Duke was scheduled to play the University of Michigan in the semi-finals. Michigan had five freshmen, dubbed the "Fab Five," who were considered the hottest players in the college game at the time. There was no question that individually they were more talented than the Duke athletes, even though they were freshman. Everyone expected them to win. In one of the best-coached games I have seen, Duke surprised the nation by beating the "Fab Five." Duke played as a team, while the spotlight-grabbing Michigan athletes couldn't get out of their own way.

Just as in sports, the cultures of different companies can reward internal loyalty and support or, alternatively, promote competition among employees. I have experienced both sides of this coin in the workplace. When I took a position at Andersen Consulting as Director of Knowledge Management, I inherited some existing employees and I hired others to make up the business unit. I created a group of very talented professionals who had the promise of great achievement.

But I quickly realized that many of the team members just didn't get it. They didn't understand that we would succeed only by supporting each other and working together as a group. There was so much infighting, back-stabbing, and whining about petty grievances that it took us twice as long to get anything done as it should have. It also made everyone, including me, appear less competent. I had a difficult time fostering teamwork and loyalty.

At the same company, I subsequently led another team that consisted of people who were aware of the importance of loyalty to the team. They supported each other and me in every way. They pointed out others' strengths rather than their weaknesses. This team ended up hitting a home run for the firm. They were viewed not only as the paragon of how an internal business unit should operate but also were recognized individually for their efforts. They received more lucrative salary increases and quicker promotions. A little loyalty went a long way.

For the most part, private wealth management firms line up squarely on one side or the other of the support versus competition continuum. I have friends at one firm that is so internally competitive the employees lock up their desks and files when they go home at night, not to prevent theft from an outside intruder but rather from an inside colleague. They are afraid that their fellow money managers will steal their clients, contacts, and leads. This organization has understandably high turnover.

Homrich Berg, a money management firm on whose advisory board I serve, takes a different approach. While each client has a primary partner with whom he or she interacts, these partners don't "own" the clients. The partners work together to maximize the income for all by sharing ideas and strategies. There are no turf wars and hoarding of knowledge. I have chosen to do business with them.

Most executive search firms, aka "head hunters," work under the same premise as money managers. Most search professionals at the well-known firms are in essence renting a desk. Every professional has his or her own book of business and clients. They are mini-entrepreneurs who benefit from the big name and reputation of the firm on their business cards. Understandably, internal competition is intense. Sometimes, two teams from the same firm will pitch the same client, vying against each other as if they were external competitors.

Joel Koblentz, a former partner with the internationally recognized search firm Egon Zehnder, feels there is a better way. He started his own company, The Koblentz Group, that is still in the search business but operates differently. He fosters collaboration among his partners by having all revenues go into one pot that is split equally among the team at year end. None of his employees works on commission. They are more consultative, less purely transactional. "We work seamlessly," Koblentz states, "and 100 percent of our engagements close." This is generally not the case with the big name firms. Seems like good business to me.

American businesses would run much more smoothly if the professionals in them would focus their competitive energies where they belong: on their competitors. Business is no different from sports; once a team is created, employees with good business savvy work to unite the individuals and capitalize on their strengths.

If one member isn't the best in front of clients, maybe she can do the behind-the-scenes work. If another doesn't like crunching numbers, put him in charge of the creative piece. It is important to present a united front to your customers and your competition. Make them believe that you have the best team going. When the players lose focus because they are constantly fighting internal battles and jockeying for position, everyone loses.

If you find yourself caught in a corporate culture that doesn't promote teamwork and fosters internal competition, you have a decision to make. You will probably not be able to change the situation within the company unless you are at the top, so your decision becomes whether to stay and play by the rules or leave. I do not believe that organizations exhibiting intense internal competition are healthy environments for any worker, male or female. You have a choice.

- *Commit to competing in a tough, male environment.*

I have always lived by the maxim that no goal is out of my reach. Early in my tennis career, my peers thought I was crazy for setting my sights high. I ended up attaining everything I had set out to achieve and more. From my years in sports, I learned that if I truly committed myself to something, I could achieve it. I also learned that it's a lot easier to give up and lose than to put forth the effort it takes to win.

I am not a great athlete; when I was competing in tennis tournaments as a teenager, I was envious of those who could effortlessly glide up to the net and execute the perfect drop volley. I apparently was not present when that kind of talent was doled out. However, I often was ranked higher than these elite athletes solely because I wanted to win more than they did. I practiced harder and was willing to hit yet one more ball to win a point when others had already given up. In my experience, the person who wants it more will get it—in both sports and business.

When I entered the world of business, I brought these same beliefs with me. The major difference was that I now had to compete with men. The environment was tougher. My first experience out of business school, when I worked for Salomon Brothers in the elite corporate finance group, was a case in point. It hit me like a sledgehammer when, after my first few months on the job, I realized that my male counterparts wanted to succeed more than I did; they felt that this was their turf. They ate, slept, breathed, and *lived* Wall Street.

During the interview process, it wasn't uncommon for the men to declare that they had dreamed of becoming investment bankers since grade school. I did not even know what an investment bank was until I got to Harvard. Now they had their life goal and I had a job. I was at an institution where the CEO was quoted in the *Wall Street Journal* as saying that we had to be ready to "bite the ass off a bear" every morning when we walked in to work. I was in the wrong place. While I relish competition and the sport of business, this level of intensity was not what I wanted for my life.

In the business world, as in sports, success means being committed to working in what may be an ultra-competitive environment that is male dominated. If you want the job, it means accepting the challenge and doing whatever it takes, even if you're outnumbered. It's having the guts to excel.

Maria Britt, a brigadier general of the Georgia Army National Guard and a graduate of The United States Military Academy, epitomizes competitiveness in a tough, male environment. As a cadet at the age of 19, she was offered the opportunity to attend the Jungle Warfare School at Ft. Sherman, Panama, becoming the first woman to be admitted. She was placed in a separate barracks that obviously hadn't been lived in for a while. It was filthy and most of the screening was torn so she was faced with "mosquitoes that were big enough to carry you away." She barricaded the door at night and slept with one eye open, feeling a slight coldness from the male, non-West Point graduates.

The first week flew by; she had no problems with the training or jungle navigation. After the first two days, helocasting was added to the instruction. This activity involved jumping out of the back of a moving helicopter at a couple hundred feet above the water in full gear, with weapon; swimming to a rubber boat; and assaulting the shore. The goal was to land at a 50-degree angle with an M16 rifle locked above your head.

Britt, however, landed at about a 30-degree angle. Impact was greater than expected and her M16 came down on the bridge of her nose, breaking it in two places and knocking her out. Fortunately, her training buddy immediately swam over, pulled her face out of the water, and flagged down the motor-boat that accompanied the exercise to rescue her. A Marine dragged her into the boat telling her not to bleed all over his white shorts. She remembers thinking he was joking. Who wears white in the jungle?

Soon Britt had company in the boat; a male classmate's M16 had landed on his upper lip, ripping it off and knocking out his two front teeth. The two of them were quite a sight, bleeding up a storm together.

The next day, other male students took a look at her and laughed. With two black eyes and a face swollen beyond recognition, she was a major attraction. During the last training meal, as she carried her dirty dishes to the conveyor belt, a man stepped in front of her and snapped a picture of her face. Her male friends wanted to jump him and pull the film out of the camera. She told them to let him have his fun; it wasn't worth getting in trouble.

A couple of months later, her roommate's boyfriend was assigned to the Jungle School. He called the girlfriend one night and said, "You won't believe what I saw yesterday. It was your roommate's picture with her broken nose and black eyes, and under the picture was written in big letters, 'This is what happens when women come to this school!'" Of course, Britt was shocked, dismayed, and infuriated.

Britt had dared to compete in one of the toughest of male environments—the military. The good news is that she succeeded. She got the badge and paved the way for other women. And that photograph is now a point of pride.

Sometimes when we choose to compete with men on their terms, we not only succeed but we also are able to change perceptions. Maria Britt did just this with an incident unrelated to Jungle School.

Many years ago, she was serving at Ft. McPherson as the first female Military Police Company Commander, and more importantly, the Commander of Troops for an important ceremony. A major approached her after the long, hot ceremony and asked her if she remembered him. Of course she did; he had been her Tactical Officer, the one in charge of her training the summer before her senior year at West Point, and he had gone out of his way to make her life and that of her roommate much more difficult.

He extended their morning runs, increased the pace, and generally did anything he could do to make them look bad in front of their peers and subordinates. Fortunately, Britt and her roommate were in top shape and the only ones dropping out of the runs were men.

Britt hadn't seen him again until this hot day at Ft. McPherson. "Yes, sir, I remember you," she said. The look on her face said much more.

He then told her that he didn't think women should have been allowed into West Point, and he had vowed to do his part to drum them out. But then he added, "I'm sorry. I shouldn't have treated you that way and I now see I was wrong about women in the military. You changed my mind." He shook her hand and walked off.

Maria Britt is one of those women competing in a male environment, succeeding, and therefore helping other women by moving history forward one person at a time.

- **Pick players based on ability**

Donna Lopiano of the Women's Sports Foundation agrees that athletes understand the basic rules of play. One of her basic rules is "teams are chosen based on people's strengths and competencies rather than who is liked or disliked." The same holds true for business.

When I was about eight years old, the neighborhood kids used to play a game called Kick the Can. It's like hide and seek, and the player who can get home and kick the can frees the prisoners.

The first time I was captain, I picked my best friend, Gracie Krause, to be a member of my team. Unfortunately for me, Gracie was not the best athlete and hence not the optimal team member, especially for my first pick. It would have been more prudent to pick kids who could run faster or were more competitive. I quickly learned my lesson; if I wanted to win, I picked the best players, not my best friends. Later, when I was playing national tennis tournaments, I always picked a doubles partner based on her ability and ranking, not her personality.

From the time my son, Pierce, was very young, he played by this rule. From pick-up games in the schoolyard, he had learned how to choose a winning team and also that winning was what mattered. Each year Pierce had a baseball party for his birthday, and he was allowed to be captain of one of the teams. I was always amused by the fact that he would bypass his best friend, who was not a stellar athlete, and immediately zero in on the best player as his first choice. What was particularly interesting was that his friend didn't fault my son's decision. This surprised me. While I might have expected Pierce to choose friendship over athleticism, I also expected his friend to be upset not to be chosen first. However, I realized later that both boys had learned exactly what I had in my kickball days—that the object of any game is to win and friendship has little to do with it. They were both already playing by one of my identified rules of engagement.

The workplace is no different. Time and again I have seen unlikely personality combinations work very well in a business setting because each is bringing his or her specific skill to the mix. Often, these team members do not interact socially because they aren't best friends. Their arrangement is strictly business.

Christine Owens, a senior vice president at UPS, prefers to surround herself with those who are smarter than she is or who have a skill set she lacks. As she says, "The more clubs you have in your bag, the better your score will be." She doesn't want to go into the tournament underclubbed.

It's important, however, to recognize that while business is not a popularity contest, people don't enjoy working for or with people they dislike. If you act like a jerk, you won't be asked back on the team, no matter how good you are.

A man I worked with at Andersen Consulting is a prime example. He was coming up for promotion to partner, and even though he was widely acknowledged as the expert in various areas of strategic consulting, nobody wanted to work with him or for him. He was abrasive, condescending, and difficult to be around. Far from encouraging his peers and subordinates, he constantly found fault with them. None of his direct reports tried to make him look good; they just tried to get off his team. Because of his personality and attitude, it took him much longer to make partner than it should have. I learned through observing him and others that if you treat others well in the workplace, they usually will return the favor.

- ### *Apply for the quarterback/pitcher positions*

If I mention Eli Manning in football or Randy Johnson in baseball, everyone knows who I'm talking about. However, most of you probably haven't heard of Devin Hester, a kicker for the Chicago Bears and one of the top ten All-Star vote-getters for the 2008 NFL Pro Bowl Team, or Joe Mauer, a catcher for Minneapolis named to the 2008 MLB All-Star game. Even though they are superstars in the same sports as Manning and Johnson respectively, only serious fans know their names.

My friends who don't follow professional sports know only the names of quarterbacks or pitchers. These players hold the most visible positions on their teams and therefore usually generate more in endorsement money than the others. Adoring fans wear their jerseys, and kids across the country aspire to be them because they wield power.

Business is no different. Positions within an organization are not created equal, even if they are at the same level. Every company has jobs that mirror quarterbacks and pitchers from a visibility standpoint. While these positions may vary from one organization to the next, they have one thing in common: they catapult workers into the executive suite.

You can easily identify these positions by checking out those who are currently in power and tracing their paths to success. What roles did they hold along the way and for how long? In many organizations, line experience is a *de facto* requirement for CEO and other executive-level jobs. Catalyst calls these line positions the "gateway for promotion to top leadership." The perception is that those with this kind of background drive the business forward.

It is not surprising, then, that most line roles are held by men. According to Catalyst, in 2007, only 27 percent of female corporate officers held line positions, compared to 50 percent of their male counterparts. Furthermore, from 2006 to 2007, the number of women in line positions actually decreased.

Line vs. Staff Positions of Fortune 500 Corporate Officers

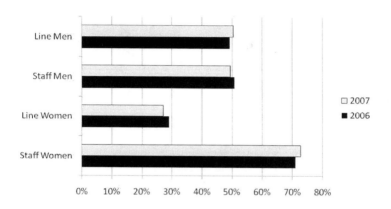

Source: Catalyst, Inc

The line positions that can do so much to advance a person's career come with a reality that is scary for many women. Because the positions have higher visibility, they carry a higher degree of risk. Even though both men and women may have their eyes on the reward, men are less afraid to take the requisite risk.

- ***Don't be afraid to make mistakes***

Babe Ruth hit 714 home runs in his lifetime, was the first player to hit 60 home runs in one season, and has been named one of the greatest baseball players in history. He also struck out 1,330 times, a career strike-out average of 24 per cent, while the most mediocre batters struck out only 12 percent of the time.

There are two lessons from Ruth's record:
(1) It's OK to make mistakes as long as you also do other things well.
(2) Don't be afraid to go for it. Everyone who plays sports knows that if you are afraid of making mistakes, your fear will keep you from winning.

During one Little League season, my son was lucky enough to have Gip Johnston, a former minor league baseball player, as his coach. Gip *knew* the game of baseball. He took a group of 11-and 12-year-olds who weren't all great athletes and molded them into the best team in the league.

As I watched the team play over a three-month period, I understood why these boys were winning more games than the others. It wasn't because they had the best hitters, infielders, or pitchers. It was because they weren't afraid to make mistakes. They played to win rather than to keep from losing. There is a subtle distinction between the two: one is surrounded by confidence, competitive spirit, and will to win. The other is paralyzed by fear of losing. It is easier to win when you don't fear losing. Indeed, it is a well-known fact that "prevent defense" in professional football loses more games than it wins. Even at this level, playing not to lose is dangerous.

In the workplace, it is also necessary to make mistakes so you can learn. In fact, Christine Owens of UPS believes failure is actually a companion of success. You can conduct practice drills for only so long. At some point you need to play for real. What you do with your failures and what you learn from them is far more important than the fact that you failed. She also advises, "If you're going to fail, you should fail boldly." Many wildly successful people have had spectacular failures in their careers. Those failures seem to make their later achievements even grander.

My favorite success to failure to success story is that of Steve Jobs. Many accounts have been written about him and his career. He and Steve Wozniak founded Apple Computer with $1,300 in start-up funding raised by selling Jobs' microbus and Wozniak's calculator. They sold circuit boards to make money while working on a personal computer prototype and finally went to market with the Apple II. In one of the most phenomenal corporate success stories in U.S. history, the Apple II's revenues soared from $2.7 million in 1977 to $200 million by 1980. However, Jobs' meteoric rise did not last long. The failure of the Macintosh, introduced in 1984, signaled the beginning of Jobs' downfall at Apple; he resigned from the company in 1985.

Jobs clearly did not want to end his career on a down note, so a few years later he introduced the NeXT computer at a lavish gala in San Francisco. As we all know, the NeXT failed miserably. One would have thought that this failure would have marked the end of Steve Jobs' career. Not so. In 1986, Jobs purchased a small company from filmmaker George Lucas. The company, called Pixar, specialized in computer animation.

Nine years later, Pixar released *Toy Story* and other box office blockbusters. One of them, *Monsters, Inc.*, had the largest opening-weekend ticket sales of any animated film in history. From a spectacular failure came phenomenal achievement, especially when one takes into account that in 2000, Jobs rejoined Apple and was once again named CEO of the now very successful company.

More women than men tend to shy away from taking risks, accepting the high-visibility job, or asking for the promotion. Many of us lack the self-assurance to believe that we can succeed in the long run even if we make mistakes, sometimes big ones, along the way. To win, women must get comfortable with failure.

- *Understand the motivations of your coaches and teammates*

There is a reason that professional athletes' betting on their own games is illegal: it alters their motivation. If an athlete receives greater compensation from throwing a game than from winning it, the competitiveness of sport is lost.

Pete Rose, a former Major League Baseball player, is famous for more than just his athletic prowess. His career is overshadowed by the fact that he was accused of betting on his sport. Rose had great ability: he played for the Cincinnati Reds for many years, is the all-time Major League leader in at bats (14,053), outs (10,328), hits (4,256) and games played

(3,562); his team won the World Series three times, and he personally made seventeen All-Star appearances at five different positions, won three batting titles, two Gold Gloves, and was Rookie of the Year.

But Pete Rose has been denied entry into the Baseball Hall of Fame solely because he gambled on his sport. The accusations claim that he bet on and against his own team, the Cincinnati Reds, while playing for or managing them. All of his wondrous achievements pale in comparison to this infraction.

The problem with Rose's betting on his sport? In any given game, nobody knew what Rose's motivation was. Did he want his team to win as any player or manager would? Or did he want his team to lose due to the large amounts of money that he would glean from his bets? The Baseball Hall of Fame took this transgression so seriously that they formally voted to ban any player who was on the "permanently ineligible" list—meaning they were disallowed from ever playing professional baseball again— from induction into the organization.

Unfortunately, there are no such rules in the workplace. While shareholders of public companies and owners of private companies try to ensure that the executive team shares their goals, it doesn't always work. Different people often have different motivations, both personal and professional, that affect how they act and react in given situations.

I recently worked with a company whose top executives clearly wanted to satisfy personal needs rather than to do what was right for the company's owners. The private equity firm's owners expected the executive team to increase EBITDA (Earnings Before Income Tax, Depreciation, and Amortization) so that the company would be more attractive for sale as quickly as possible. However, not all of the senior leaders shared this motivation.

The VP of Operations' motivation was directly in line with that of the owners. He wanted to improve the bottom line immediately to get the best price for the company and collect his approximately $2 million as soon as possible (i.e., when the company was sold).

The CFO's story was quite different. He was in his mid-50s, had two children out of college—and a three-year-old son from his second wife. He wanted this position and employment to be his last, yet he didn't feel that the $2 million ownership stake he would receive upon the company's sale would last him through raising a young son, paying for college, and covering other expenses. It also was likely that when the company sold, he would be out of a job. He therefore preferred to have the company sell five or so years in the future. He would then receive his nice salary for a few more years, collect his payout, and retire. The timing was just not quite right now.

The CEO had a third motivation. He wanted to be part of the team that would be the next purchaser of the company. He therefore understood the need to improve EBITDA, but maybe he didn't want it to improve too much. It was actually beneficial for him if the company sold at a lower price now and a higher price later, when he had a larger equity stake.

Employees without knowledge of these executives' competing motivations would be confused by their actions. In this case, pleasing their boss might have been in direct conflict with what the owners of the company wanted. Most men know exactly where their loyalty lies because they were trained early to obey your coach, obey your boss, or suffer the consequences. They figure out quickly what their direct supervisor wants. I encourage women to do the same: to understand who wants what and why. Then you can decide if you want to play the game or not. This in turn puts us squarely at the last rule of engagement.

- ***Know when to play, when to just say no, and the consequences of both***

Many years ago, a friend of mine, Mike Shapiro, was playing a tennis tournament at a country club that was very upper crust and did not admit Jewish members. Mike, who is Jewish, was playing against one of the club's own. A few games into the match, it became clear that his opponent was cheating on line calls. To add insult to injury, the crowd was cheering for it, and Mike was refused an umpire when he requested one.

Although Mike was convinced that anti-Semitism was rearing its ugly head, there was nothing he could do about it. "I finally realized that if I hit a ball within a foot of any line, my opponent would call it out so I just aimed for the center," he said.

On match point in Mike's favor, his opponent hit a ball squarely into the middle of the court. Mike caught the ball in his hand, called it out–even though it was clearly in—and walked off the court with a victory. Everyone was speechless.

There are a couple of actions that Mike could have taken when he realized he was in a situation he felt was wrong. He could have complained to tournament officials and refused to play, or he could have continued to play, knowing that in this case the rules were unfair and unethical. Whenever someone else is making us play a game that we don't like or that we feel compromises our values, we have the option to play or leave. Mike decided to play and get his vindication by winning.

When you feel uncomfortable with the culture or dissatisfied with the operation of an organization, you can leave. Nobody can force you to stay and play by the company's rules. You might choose to stay, but sometimes you might choose to exit the field. There are consequences of either choice.

In the late 1990s, I was in London at my company's executive committee meeting. I was one of two females present and one of the more junior members in a group of about 20 men. Following the first night's dinner, the senior members of the team suggested that we regroup for after-dinner drinks. Despite having jet lag and wanting to sleep, I went along because I knew that the rules dictated I should be part of this bonding session.

The drinking establishment picked by the senior executives was called Stringfellows and featured "exotic dancing." In other words, the club was an upscale strip joint. I was not aware of this fact until I stepped inside and realized that my female colleague and I were the only two women in the place who were wearing clothes. I was unwittingly taking part in an inappropriate extra-curricular entertainment that this company—and many others—condoned.

In the past, men hadn't had to contend with female executives and often favored macho activities that emphasized the very masculine nature of business itself. Interestingly, even though they now had women present, they obviously hadn't given that fact a second thought. What made the whole experience even more humiliating was that I had not been warned about the nature of the entertainment before agreeing to attend.

This is a perfect example of a game I did not want to play and thought the company should not allow. In this situation, I decided to just say no to the activity, but not to the company. I felt it was my obligation to try to rewrite the rules rather than to resign.

I spoke to the managing partner about the inappropriateness of the incident. He was duly embarrassed, and the company now does not allow company-sanctioned events to be held in establishments like Stringfellows.

"Stringfellows-gate" went against the way the game is usually played (shut up if you're in the minority), but in this case I felt that it was my responsibility to speak up and deal with the negative consequences.

Attempting to rewrite the rules is always risky business and sometimes a slippery slope. I have had junior women tell me that they are going to change the world of business by not conforming to the culture of their organizations. They are going to shake things up and change the order to fit what they think is right.

I suggest that unless there is something unethical or illegal going on, you ignore the rules at your peril. It is only the exceptional woman or man who can change a company's culture from the bottom up. When you get into the executive suite, you will have much more influence over how your company plays the game. Until then, do what you feel you must, but be aware of what the consequences might be.

This does not mean that I advocate staying in a situation that feels like fingernails on a chalkboard. My personal credo is this: If you are unhappy with the way things are done, ask yourself two questions. The first is, "Can I change things?" If the answer is yes, then make the change(s), stay at your company, and be happy.

If the answer is no, you ask yourself the second question, which is, "Can I live with the way things are?" If the answer is yes, then stay and stop griping. If the answer is no, then leave. I never advocate staying in any organization that is abusive or unethical or where you simply don't feel comfortable. There will always be another job.

I also caution people to look closely at their current situation. The devil you know may be better than the devil you don't. More than once I have left an employer thinking I was moving on to a much better environment, only to learn that my new job had its own set of annoying peculiarities.

The equal-opportunity leveler

Throughout this chapter I have talked about sports, rules and competition. While I think that an understanding of sports can be a clear advantage in business, I do not believe that playing sports is the only way to climb the corporate ladder. The Lucky Seven rules are not all sports related.

I also do not believe that women are the only ones who are sometimes negatively affected by their lack of sports knowledge or participation. The benefits one enjoys in the workplace from an interest or ability in sports are gender neutral. If a company's culture is extremely sports oriented, ignorance of or lack of interest in sports can negatively affect men as well as women. I have a very intelligent male friend who does not enjoy organized sports. He does not watch football, baseball or basketball, and he doesn't follow the stats.

He has confided to me that at times this lack of information puts him at a disadvantage in business situations. He has to work harder to be part of the team, but he is unwilling to compromise who he is for the sake of getting ahead. Although he is successful, I always wonder how much more successful he would be if he played the game like one of the guys.

While I have worked with or managed many men who are, indeed, comfortable with the game, I also have managed some who, like my friend, have not read the playbook. I have known that their career paths would be rocky if they continued to work in an office culture that relied heavily on participation in or knowledge of sports.

I have also worked with women who have done their homework and scouted the landscape of their office culture. When that culture included sports, they were actually more successful than their non-athletic male counterparts in effectively maneuvering around the field. These women are headed for success.

Quick Tip

If you really feel uninformed about sports and are therefore shying away from taking your client to the company box or afraid to accept an invitation yourself, consider signing up for a "Sports 101" workshop. Yes, Virginia, there really are such workshops. Boston-based Diane Darling, a consultant who ordinarily runs business-oriented workshops that teach people to expand and leverage their network of professional contacts, organizes an event called Water Cooler Football. Attendees pay $35 to spend two hours being tutored by former Patriots tight end Paul Francisco.

Darling says she routinely encounters people who turn down invitations to watch football games because they're afraid of appearing ignorant. "They'd say, 'I'm missing out on networking opportunities I think would be good for me,'" Darling says.

Think of a workshop such as Water Cooler Football as a new way to make contacts and carry on an interesting non-business conversation. The next time a colleague in your office talks about how great the Dallas Cowboys' defense was in yesterday's game, you'll know what they mean. And that can only be good.

Chapter Six:
LUCKY SEVEN RULE 2: HELP OTHER WOMEN ... AND MEN

"There is a special place in hell for women who don't help other women." – *Madeleine Albright*

In 1979, when I was just out of college, I thought I had hit the big time when I landed a job in the data processing division of IBM. I was hired to sell large mainframe computers at a starting salary of $16,000 a year, more money than I had ever thought I could earn.

In my first few months on the job, a seemingly inconsequential experience taught me a big lesson I have carried with me to this day. A friend from outside IBM came to me for help. He asked me for some information I could get easily from the IBM library. It was public knowledge, so helping him wouldn't compromise any ethical code.

However, at the time, I didn't understand how the game was played: that if I assisted him now, he would owe me one in the future. All I could think of was that his request would eat into the precious time I was devoting to learning about how to sell computers. I stalled.

He answered my reluctance by going to one of my male co-workers, who readily got him the information he wanted. I was dumbfounded. Why would my colleague spend his valuable time helping a person who wasn't even a good friend of his? The answer, of course, is that this is what business is all about. Men, more or less faithfully, help other men. They help friends with networking connections, hire colleagues they know, and promote their own. Men understand the value of helping others.

After this lesson, I got it, too. I understood that assisting friends and acquaintances is critical to business success because it is an essential part of networking. I could not and did not want to ignore it. I now make point of always trying to help others, women or men, when I can. I have met with clients' children who are interested in applying to Harvard or Duke; I have counseled those looking for a job or a business introduction to a contact of mine; I have played numerous sets of tennis with those I ordinarily might not have considered opponents or partners. I have also had more glasses of wine and more meals than I care to admit—all in the name of helping someone else.

I am not alone in doing all of this. Our brothers in the workforce do it every day. They understand the basic tenet of business: what goes around comes around. They know how important it is to build relationships, especially loyal ones. Even when they leave a company, they make sure that they keep in touch with their former colleagues.

The notion of helping others is so ingrained in the way business is conducted it can often be a business unto itself. Let's go back to the example of Lisa Henderson. She learned early in her soccer career that you help your teammates and they in turn help you. Her first venture, Leveledge.com, was built on this premise. Her goal was to build a business that helped young athletes find their way to college just as she had. Besides monetary income, who knows what else Henderson got in return?

In January of 2000, the Forum For Women Entrepreneurs and the National Women's Business Council teamed up to host Springboard 2000, a one-day venture capital forum devoted solely to female entrepreneurs; 350 women-led businesses applied for 27 spots. The participants represented a broad range of companies in the business-to-business, business-to-consumer, wireless, and even biotechnology areas. Today, Springboard Enterprises is *the* go-to organization for information about and support for emerging growth ventures led by women. And it fills a long-vacant niche.

The profile of the female entrepreneur has gone through a couple of iterations over the past twenty years. "Traditional" women entrepreneurs prior to the 1980s had liberal arts backgrounds and were not likely to start their businesses in male-dominated industries. They tended to be sole proprietors of small, low-income service businesses with low earnings and few assets. They generally did not possess the education or the business experience of their fellow male entrepreneurs. These traditional women entrepreneurs owned fewer than one million firms.

By 1997, women ran 9 million businesses with revenues of $3 trillion and a work force of 27 million according to the U.S. Census Bureau. The growth rate of women-led businesses was twice the rate of their male counterparts and the industries they were choosing to enter were the "non-traditional sectors" such as finance, manufacturing, and technology. Further research revealed, however, that while access to capital sources had improved for women-led businesses, women did not have adequate access to the equity capital necessary to finance these non-traditional businesses. According to Venture One, only 1.7 percent of the billions in venture capital investments made in 1997 had been invested in women-led businesses. This is the environment in which the Springboard founders felt they could make a difference. They could not only teach these female entrepreneurs new skills but also could give them access to capital.

By 2004, an estimated 47.7 percent (10.6 million) of all privately held businesses in the U.S. were 50 percent or more owned by women and generated $2.46 trillion in sales. Springboard has become a central player in the infrastructure that fosters women's entrepreneurship with the goal of connecting women entrepreneurs and investors nationally and globally. What began as a series of Venture Capital Forums seeded and promoted by hundreds of supporters has proven to be a highly effective model for fast-tracking women entrepreneurs into the equity markets. Women's desire to do our own thing has always been there; the opportunity has not. The people running Springboard are making their living by helping women get ahead in business.

While helping others is important, it is just one piece of the greater skill known as networking. Networking is the way businesspeople build their support groups for the future. While it is an essential part of business, it can also take a lot of time. I break networking down into three action steps: 1)Decide who you want in your network, 2)Discover the most effective way to reach new entrants, and 3) Priority-rank your activities.

- **Decide who you want in your network.**

From a business perspective, it is most important that you reach out to and maintain relationships with those who can help you in some way. They may be able to help you directly if they can offer you a job or get you on a board, or their help may be indirect: introducing you to someone who can then help you directly. One group represents those you want to meet and the other is the connector to those people. These roles often change over time. Someone who is of direct help to you today may change jobs tomorrow and become a connector to a new group.

My current network consists of an eclectic group of men and women of all ages I can call on for favors; they in turn feel they can call on me. I make a point of keeping in touch with them, even if it's not in person and even if I am not in need of a favor. It is very difficult to ask contacts for help when you haven't reached out to them in years and you do so only when you need them. They feel used and may be less willing to help. Make sure you regularly cultivate your current network.

In addition to tending to my current network, I am also constantly searching for new entrants: high profile individuals; up-and-comers; and other bright, energetic, fun people that I know will add value to my group of friends and colleagues.

Not everyone feels the need to add to their collection of contacts. I have a friend who grew up in Atlanta, is a member of one of the most prestigious country clubs in the area, and is definitely part of the moneyed social scene. She once told me that she just didn't have room for any more friends; her life was complete. I find that sad. I *never* want my world to be complete in that respect. It has served me well to keep myself open to new people and new possibilities.

- **Discover the most effective way to reach new entrants**

Once you have determined the individuals or type of people you would like to add to your network, the trick is to figure out how to reach them. If there are friends of friends you would like to meet, an introduction is the best way to go, followed up by a one-to-one meeting. Often a person's level in an organization dictates how much time you can co-opt for that first meeting. I have found that the higher up the totem pole the individual is, the more difficult it is to get him or her to commit to a precious lunch hour meeting. Luckily, God invented coffee bars, which is a meeting option almost any time of the day.

If there is a particular group you want to get involved with, attend seminars and networking events where you know you'll find those people. For example, when I first moved to Atlanta, I felt that it would be good to be plugged in to the Harvard Business School alumni network. I started attending their Breakfast Series events, where Atlanta business leaders spoke once a month; I volunteered to be on a women's panel. Now, years later, some of my best friends and contacts are Harvard alumni in the Atlanta area.

Networking events and groups are not just based on educational affiliations. Groups that pull people with common business, community, sports, or other interests are all fair game. Joining not-for-profit boards or signing up for volunteer opportunities can be a great way to build your network—and to make permanent friends who share your passions. If you are a tri-athlete, join the local Tri club; if you are a runner, the local track club is sure to yield some new friends. You'd be surprised at the number of high-level executives who have the same interests you do.

Enhance new relationships by going above and beyond business lunches and networking events. Get tickets to a sporting event or cultural activity that your prospect enjoys. Host a dinner party at your home and invite new contacts as well as old friends. There is no right way to network; whatever works for you is right.

Melissa Marek Babb, a managing director with Harbert Management Corporation, a $16 billion asset management firm, is a master at business networking. When she moved to Atlanta from New York, she didn't know one person except those with whom she had interviewed in her office. Many New York friends asked her what they could do to help. She said, "Just introduce me to one person you think I should meet, whether they're interesting, a college roommate, well-connected in the business world, involved in the arts, or just plain fun."

She followed up promptly on each introduction, sent an e-mail, and took the person out to breakfast or arranged a coffee meeting. Her objective in that first meeting was to briefly cover her career background and enough personal information so that her new contact might consider other people Melissa would be interested in meeting. Nearly every introduction resulted in two more.

Melissa also made a specific promise to herself that when she arrived in Atlanta she would follow up on casual introductions. Each time she chatted with someone interesting at a cocktail party, business meeting, or other venue, she would ask for a business card and contact him or her within a week. No more business cards languishing in a drawer for six months!

She found that the follow-up would usually surprise people. Once again, she would suggest a breakfast meeting or a coffee. This turned casual introductions into meaningful dialogue and, ultimately, new friends and connections.

Melissa also does a fantastic job at entertaining. She feels that at-home entertaining is much more personal and powerful than an invitation to go out to a restaurant. When planning a party at her house, she tries to invite a group of people/couples who don't know each other but should. Business acquaintances turn into friends. She actually keeps a running list of people she would like to invite to her home. Before the event, she sends an e-mail with one or two sentences about each person's background or business affiliations. By serving as a master connector of intriguing people, Melissa becomes top of mind with a lot of influential people who will undoubtedly stay part of her network.

A host of technology-related networking tools has recently come into vogue. Services such as LinkedIn and Facebook are now used by businesspeople across the country and the world. I was surprised when I received an e-mail from Bain & Company announcing the launch of their alumni network on both of these Web sites—but I shouldn't have been. I thought Facebook was just for my college-aged children, but it's not. Services such as these have become mainstream and are worth joining. It only takes a few minutes to create your profile, it's free, and there could be a payback. In the e-mail that Bain sent out, the pitch to the alumni was, "Want to find and reconnect with friends and former coworkers, view classic Bain videos, and discover inside connections that can help you land jobs and close deals? Click on the links below to get started!" That worked for me.

- **Priority-rank your activities.**

The great thing about networking is that if you do it right, you will enrich both your business life and your personal life by frequently adding new friends and acquaintances. The downside is that it takes time. My advice is to priority-rank your activities based on cost and payback and to manage your budget. Although it sounds calculating, you must think about the payback of each activity on which you embark.

Most high-level executives can attend a different activity every day of the week if they so choose—and some are mandatory. These professionals pick carefully, not for budget reasons, but because of constraints on their time. Most junior professionals have the time but not the money to attend everything. If you can get your company to pay for networking activities, wonderful. If not, choose events or memberships that give you the biggest bang for the buck and make yourself known.

Even though we're learning fast, women have historically not been as good at networking as men. Many women simply don't understand the power of a strong network and that the way to build that network is to be the one who helps someone else first.

Unfortunately, our naiveté has led to what I feel are unfounded claims that women don't help other women in business. We hear that we're our own worst enemies and that once we've made it in the corporate world, we let other women fend for themselves.

This fiction is often cited as one of the reasons women have not made greater strides in the workplace. I have been part of corporate America for more years than I care to admit and have been in very competitive environments. While I was often one of only a few professional females in my office, I never experienced the myth of women not helping women. In fact, if it weren't for some of my female managers and mentors, my road to success probably would have been a lot more difficult.

I feel certain that the situation for women is not very different from that of men. Men help men much of the time, but not always. We all know how competitive men can be, and I have witnessed numerous occasions in which they not only didn't help other men but openly sabotaged them, especially if the two were in competition for the same job, a raise, or a promotion.

Similarly, women often help other women, but not always. In the midst of the daily battle we call business, women can compete with the best of them—and sometimes have to compete against each other. Anyone who has been in a sales position or within the politics of a corporation knows that it is often survival of the fittest. In most competitive instances, each competitor will vie to edge out the closest rival, regardless of gender. It's interesting, then, that it never occurs to anyone to announce that men don't help men. Perhaps the reality is that men understand the game better and are able to give the illusion of supporting each other. And perhaps women can do better than that. Maybe we really can help each other–and the men too.

Quick Tips

Work your existing contacts. Go through your Rolodex® or contact list in Outlook® and make a list of those people that you want to stay in touch with on a regular basis. Reach out to each one via e-mail or phone with a quick update on what you're doing. With some, you may want to schedule a breakfast or lunch. With others, the e-mail or phone call will suffice. Perhaps there is an article or book you have read lately that would interest them either personally or professionally. It is important that you are not asking them for a favor, simply catching up and looking for opportunities to help others. Continue to stay in touch on whatever schedule you feel is appropriate or they dictate—and always update your list with new contacts. The next time you need a favor, you will have many places to turn.

Make new contacts. At a minimum, create a LinkedIn profile. Invite everyone in your Outlook contacts to join. You will gain new contacts as others ask you to join their networks. When you want to connect with someone you don't know, check LinkedIn and see if one of your contacts knows that person. Then don't be afraid to ask for an introduction. Most of your friends and business colleagues will be happy to accommodate.

Chapter Seven
LUCKY SEVEN RULE 3:
APPLY TO THE GOOD OLD
BOY NETWORK. TODAY.

"I don't care to belong to a club that accepts people like me as members." – Groucho Marx

Ask Martha Burk, former chairwoman of the National Council of Women's Organizations, and she will tell you that the Good Old Boy network is alive and well at Augusta National Golf Club. In 2003, Burk famously led a Masters week demonstration outside Augusta National to protest the club's male-only membership policy.

Whether it is Augusta National or another male bastion, any kind of discrimination based on gender, race, or religion is deplorable. But this type of exclusion is particularly harmful to businesswomen. If we can't rub elbows with the power group in and out of the workplace, women experience yet one more disadvantage or obstacle to success. Women often have a more difficult time getting these elbow-rubbing opportunities. High achieving women take those opportunities when they can. Carly Fiorina, one of the "fearless female CEOs" from Chapter Two, is an example of this type of woman.

Fiorina's book, *Tough Choices*, chronicles not only her life at Hewlett Packard but also her early career. After graduating from high school, Fiorina attended Stanford University in Palo Alto, California, where she majored in medieval history and philosophy. Upon graduation, she immediately enrolled in the University of California School of Law but dropped out after only one semester. She proceeded to work in a variety of jobs including secretary, receptionist and stock broker. She even taught English in Bologna, Italy when her first husband's career took them to that country. Finally, she decided to go back to school. This time, she focused on a career in business, and in 1980 earned a graduate business degree from the University of Maryland.

With her newly minted M.B.A., Fiorina accepted a job as an account executive with AT&T, working first in Washington, D.C. in the company's long–distance phone service operations. Her responsibilities included selling the company's long–distance services to government agencies. Impressed by her performance, AT&T executives identified her as a likely candidate for a management position and in 1988 sent her to the Sloan School of the Massachusetts Institute of Technology to earn a master of science degree.

It was at the Sloan School that Fiorina first met the head of AT&T's Network Systems Group, an equipment division that seemed to be going nowhere. Against the advice of friends, Fiorina switched from long–distance operations to Network Systems and almost immediately was shipped to the Far East to work on complicated joint ventures for the division. Although business negotiating in Asia is almost exclusively an all–male preserve, Fiorina found a way to fit in.

In *Tough Choices*, Fiorina details a particular incident that occurred on a trip to South Korea where she made the decision to flout convention in order to fit in. Foreign businessmen visiting South Korea traditionally are treated to a *kisaeng* party, where their dinner companions are the equivalent of geishas. Women are never invited. But Fiorina was. Her hosts offered a male companion but Fiorina said did not want them to make special arrangements on her account. She would accept the treatment normally afforded a Korean business colleague.

And that is exactly what she got—the usual *kisaeng* treatment of food, drink and a female dinner companion. As it turns out, Fiorina's companion proved respectful and instrumental in helping Fiorina understand the traditions—complete with drinking game—of a kisaeng dinner.

Fiorina could have been embarrassed and refused to participate in this bonding. However, she knew that by accepting the same treatment as the men—treatment that did not cross any ethical boundaries—she would be taking a huge step toward being accepted and viewed as one of the guys, in the most positive sense; she also would be helping her clients feel comfortable. Given the power structure at AT&T, this was a good move for Fiorina. Her attitude and ability to seize opportunities for acceptance into the boys' network served her well in her career. She ultimately captured the top spot in a Fortune 500 company operating in the technology industry—very much a male preserve.

There may be times when you just want to beat the good old boy network—into oblivion perhaps—but this is not the answer. I am an optimist. I know that the good old boy network exists, but I believe women can and will be admitted, not by staging protests but by being accepted as Fiorina was in Korea. During my many years in business, I have used different tactics to gain entry. However, my first order of business is always to figure out where I should focus my acceptance-gaining efforts.

Whenever I join a new company or organization, I quickly determine who has the power and who owns the influence. Someone once told me that politics exist in every business setting that involves more than one person, and he was right. Since politics are a big part of playing the business game, understanding them within your organization is always critical to advancement and sometimes to survival. It seems that at all levels within a company, there are those with whom others want to be associated—the "cool kids' table," if you will. The in-group consists of those who are already in positions of power, plus their chosen friends, and is almost all male. They rely on each other for promotions, support, introductions, and anything else that will help them get ahead in the organization.

Outside of a company, there are in-groups and out-groups as well, but they are not always so clearly defined. Here the in-group, again mostly male, includes those who are plugged in to the community and have the best connections. These people help each other by making introductions, proposing each other for memberships in the right clubs, and getting each other on high-visibility corporate or not-for-profit boards. They even help each other move from one company to another when in job-search mode. Because of their influence, they are able to make things happen for their friends.

Each city has its own power system that may take some sleuthing to identify. One large New York bank attempting to tackle the Atlanta business market actually hired a firm to perform a "city study" to determine how the power structure in Atlanta operated. They wanted to make sure they hit the ground running when they opened an Atlanta office.

The firm concluded that Atlanta's movers and shakers did their networking on not-for-profit boards and that not all not-for-profits were created equal; some carried more cachet than others. The bank labeled these "must participate" boards and promptly divided them up among the executives in the territory, giving them a year to make it onto the board. In this case, the bank paid big money solely to identify the network they wanted to join, but you can do the same by asking your networks for help.

People in general have a tendency to favor the in-group's opinions and actions. The positive characteristics of the in-group are usually exaggerated, while the negative traits of the corresponding out-group are similarly magnified. Therefore, people want to be part of the in-group, not only because the group wields more power and influence, but also because of the positive feelings of self-worth that come with having this association.

Identifying the good old boy network is not that difficult. Just look up. The hard part is gaining entry. Human behaviorists claim that we place ourselves and others in categories based not only on visible characteristics but also on our assumptions about attitudes, behavior, beliefs, and actions. We classify others on the basis of their similarities to or differences from us. In other words, I perceive others as being either in same category I inhabit or as members of a category different from mine.

We all also have our "source of pride" categories. When we can place ourselves in these categories, we feel good about ourselves. These categories can be based on any number of attributes from race to school affiliation to gender. The important thing to note is that if other people belong to a category *of which I'm proud to be a member*, I will classify them there first. I will include them in my in-group.

As you become increasingly aware of what your personal sources of pride are and how you categorize yourself and others, you will understand how others do the same.

The good old boy network is simply a business in-group whose members pride themselves on having certain attributes in common, one of them being male. The key to gaining entry to the good old boy network is to identify those common interests or core identities other than being male that make men feel good about themselves, and then to figure out how those interests or identities overlap with yours. It's not that hard to do. Good old boys have many interests that aren't gender specific:

- College
- Sports
- Personal/family
- Hobbies
- Culture/arts
- Community

One of the easiest sources of interest overlap is college. If you have the same undergraduate degree as those in the network, you can immediately use that to your advantage. I especially see this when it involves NCAA sports. For example, when basketball season rolls around, you better believe that I'm talking trash in my office as I associate myself with Duke's basketball team, which, luckily for me, has been excellent for many years.

In this case, I can identify with anyone who went to Duke, another ACC school, or another Division I school with a basketball team. The possibilities are limitless. I am immediately brought into a group that might not have included me had I not highlighted my affiliation with something that gives them a sense of pride: college sports. Most offices that I have observed or in which I have worked revolve around college sports in one way or another. An easy way to gain entry is to understand these sports, their rivalries, and power group's interest in them.

A few years ago, I was able to establish a strong relationship with one of the board members of the company where I was employed due to our common interest in college basketball. He had attended Georgia Tech as an undergraduate and was an avid fan of their sports teams. I immediately began teasing him about Duke's higher ranking in the polls. Because they are both ACC schools, the rivalry was intense.

When he invited me to join him in his box for the Georgia Tech/Duke game being played in Atlanta, I promised him that I would wear a "Georgia Tech gold" T-shirt. I kept my promise and wore the other team's color, but I had a special shirt created just for this game. On the pocket, in very small letters, were the words "GO DUKE." I wore the shirt to the game and the rivalry continued. He has proven to be a friend and mentor, helping me in business on more than one occasion. I would not have this relationship were it not for a joint interest.

But the common interest doesn't have to be traditional sports, and in fact doesn't have to be sports at all. It can be something fairly obscure. When I was a consultant at Bain & Company, one of the partners was really into Ultimate Frisbee. It was the late '80s and the sport was in its infancy. I had never heard of it, but it sounded like fun. So I tried it out, liked it, and became part of a growing Bain team that played on the weekends. I also developed a bond with someone I ordinarily would not have known and received a great mentor in the process.

Community activities are excellent avenues to forge a common bond. Hands On Atlanta, a non-profit organization that helps individuals, families, and corporate and community groups find flexible volunteer opportunities around the city, inadvertently offers a way for businesswomen to bond with businessmen. Many companies in the metropolitan Atlanta area sponsor volunteer activities that range from building houses to dishing soup at the local community food bank.

Many of the events are "guy friendly" and attract more men than other non-profits. For businesswomen wanting to improve their community, an organization such as Hands On Atlanta is a great way to get involved with a passion and rub elbows with businessmen who share a common interest. Go online or check the phone book for similar organizations in your city.

There are times when finding a point of entry is more difficult than others. Because of my sports background, I have generally had an easy time finding common interests with even the tightest of good old boy systems. Therefore, I was surprised a few years ago to find myself unable to connect with Mike, the head of an office of the firm where I worked. How could this happen to me, the female who was always accepted? I was the one who a male friend once jokingly dubbed "more one of the guys than the guys."

No matter what I did, I could not gain entry to Mike's group. The phrase "good old boy" was coined with him in mind. He took pride in portraying himself as a easy-going beer drinker intent on reliving his Southern college glory days, even though he was well into his forties. I felt like the Yankee he wanted to send home. Even the Duke connection didn't cut it. Mike once told me that while Duke was geographically Southern, that didn't count because all the students came from New York.

I was mulling over my dilemma when I had an epiphany. Mike talked about his children. A lot. He had pictures of them plastering his office, always made time to attend their sporting events, and talked to them frequently during the day from work. He had one child in college, as did I. Eureka! I had found my connection.

One of Mike's sources of pride was that people labeled him a great family man. At the time, my son, a freshman at the University of San Diego, was unhappy with his choice of schools and wanted to transfer to the University of Colorado. What better way to connect with Mike than to get his advice on what I should do? Our over-the-top interest in our respective children was our interest overlap. The rest was easy. I met him for lunch, talked a little shop, and then steered the conversation to my son. Our discussion was sincere and helpful to me. From that point on, my relationship with Mike was different.

I believe women gain more respect from men by identifying with their interests than by using our brains to solve a business problem. It is impossible to show how smart we are if we aren't even given the chance. If we are excluded from the club, we may find that chance elusive. While the bad news is that good old boy networks still exist, the good news is that determined women across the U.S. are gaining entry every day.

That brings me back to Brigadier General Maria Britt. She found she had gained entry through an incident that still makes her smile. About 15 years ago, she was a junior major working as a training officer for overseas deployment training. It was tough to get these missions and even tougher to get them with funding. She was determined to send one of her companies to Germany for an annual training event.

Her boss said, "Don't waste your time. Won't happen." She pursued it anyway and worked with headquarters and everyone in between to get the mission—and the dollars that went with it.

During the year she had been in her job, she'd noticed that whenever any of the men did something notable, one of the colonels would point his finger and say, "You're the man!" Maria realized he would never say, "You're the man!" to her, but that wasn't a problem. It became her private inside joke.

A few months later, she got the mission and $40,000 to support it. She mentioned the accomplishment at the next section meeting and the colonel of finger-pointing fame was excited by it. He stood up, pointed his finger at her and said, "You're the WO-man!" Everyone burst out laughing. She realized then and there that she had been wholeheartedly accepted as one of the guys–in a good way.

I believe that most people are inherently decent and don't consciously exclude others. My advice is to make the first move and never let up. You too can join the good old boys and be the "WO-man!"

Quick Tip

I recommend a couple of exercises that will help you improve your ability to join the good old boy network. Today!

Pick a man with whom you want to connect from a business perspective—preferably one who can help you professionally but who has remained elusive or non-responsive. Next, determine what that person's "source of pride" categories are and which one(s) overlap with your interests. Finally, try to connect with that person using your new knowledge and see if it makes a difference.

Start a new activity that interests you and that you think will help you from a business perspective. A friend of mine who is a lawyer for Cox Communications started taking golf lessons in her late forties after a lifetime of not focusing on any sports. Golf is now her new passion. She is enjoying learning the game and it is helping her in the workplace. She can now participate in corporate golf outings and lament or boast with office colleagues about her last great or miserable round. She is now an insider with those who view golf as one of their source of pride categories.

Chapter Eight:
LUCKY SEVEN RULE 4:
BRAND YOUR PASSION

"It doesn't matter what we expect from life, but rather what life expects from us." –Victor Frankl

Sara Blakely wanted footless bodyshaping pantyhose to wear with her cream-colored pants and open-toed shoes, but she couldn't find them anywhere. She bought clothes that in her words "looked amazing in a magazine or on the hanger, but in reality magnified every panty line and imperfection—clothes that eventually made their way to the 'maybe one day I'll be flawless' section of my closet where they remained unworn." A "door-to-door salesgirl" of copiers and office equipment, Blakely waited for the right idea to come to her and eventually hit upon it when she created the first pair of footless stockings and launched her own company—SPANX.

Two years later, after what Blakely describes as "a lot of Internet research" she had a patented product that she was able to place in top retail stores across the country. She sold more than 50,000 pairs of footless pantyhose in three months from the back of her apartment and revitalized an industry that had been languishing for ten years. By 2002, Sara was named Ernst and Young's Southeast Regional Entrepreneur of the Year. She now says, "I never dreamed visible panty lines and uncomfortable thongs would inspire me to become an inventor."

The company today has more than 50 employees, a separate brand at Target (ASSETS), and more than $150 million in retail sales. Sara's story and SPANX products have been featured on everything from CNN and Oprah to *Forbes, Glamour, Vogue, People, InStyle, The New York Times, Vanity Fair, WWD* and *USA Today.*

We can all learn from Sara Blakely. She has done an incredible job of branding herself. Her product is not simply SPANX; it is SPANX *by Sara Blakely.* She is like Richard Branson of Virgin Airways fame—a creative entrepreneur, full of adventure and with a great story.

While you may or may not realize it, you are a brand. Your brand is your promise to your customer, whether that customer is internal or external. Branding is one of the most important aspects of business because it tells your customers what they can expect from your products and services, and it differentiates your offering from your competitors'. Your brand is derived from who you are, who you want to be, and who people perceive you to be. It includes all of the intangible and emotional bonds that exist between you and those who want to buy what you have to offer.

If you don't have a personal brand, the workplace often doesn't know what to do with you. Most people feel comfortable when they can place others in a box based on ability or persona. The trick is to make sure that the box others see you in is the one you want to occupy. Managing yourself as a brand is a necessary part of business today so that you can quickly and easily define your career niche to others.

I recommend three steps to effectively brand yourself for career success: 1) Identify your platform, 2) Define your audience, and 3) Refine your message.

- **Identify your platform**

Your platform is the essence of what you do in your career. Your platform extends beyond your position at a particular firm. It can be industry focused (e.g., healthcare, retail, communications), where your strength is in knowing the industry inside and out; or it can be functionally focused (e.g., strategy, procurement, IT), where you are able to translate your functional knowledge across different industries.

Most often, I have been viewed functionally—a "strategy guru"—mainly because I worked for Bain & Company, one of the world's best-known strategy consulting firms, and subsequently for the strategic services division of Andersen Consulting (now Accenture).

I was branded by default. I encourage you, however, *not* to let others define you, but to be active in branding yourself and deciding what suits you best and what you would like the outside world to see. Your route to self-branding begins with the identification of what your personal platform is all about.

I believe you should make money from your endeavors and be happy while doing it. Therefore, to find your calling, you should consider two things: *what you do best* and *what you prefer to do*. The intersection of these two themes is a good place to start. Love what you do and do it well. If you can differentiate yourself from the pack with your skills and don't mind logging some crazy hours because you enjoy your work, you're on your way to career success.

The first question you should ask yourself is, "What do I do best?" Upon reflection, you may remember that you had very high scores on the math portion of your SAT but scored dismally on the verbal portion. You love figuring out number puzzles and discerning the patterns in mathematical problems. For you, a career that involves analysis may be the right choice. You can also look at previous jobs or extracurricular activities to find your strengths. The bottom line is that your platform or career choice should reflect your strengths.

Thinking about what your strong suits are can help you find your passion—the second part of building your branding platform. Most of us are passionate about things we do well. I believe you will be happiest in your career if you love doing what you do. Usually the money then follows.

Of course, there are many people in business today who have done well pursuing money rather than their personal passions. I went to business school with a lot of them. But most people who follow this route can't wait to retire so that they can enjoy their wealth. The sad thing is that they are deferring today's pleasure for "later." It's a shame to miss your present moments by waiting for the fun you're going to have someday. The future is often not what you expect. Things happen. Even death happens. And if you haven't enjoyed your present moments, you'll lie on your deathbed regretting what you didn't do. Don't wait to enjoy your life. Do it now by choosing a career you can love.

Each person's passion is personal. You may find yourself wanting to know everything you can about computers and information technology, or you may think that marketing is the most fascinating topic imaginable. To help you identify what gets you "jazzed," you may want to ask yourself the following questions:

- What motivates me to get up in the morning?
- What do I like about what I do?
- What would I do for free?

Many professional athletes, entertainers, and artists of various types are passionate about what they do. They have to be. The physical and emotional demands are great; injuries are common; and in the case of writers, artists, dancers, and musicians, rejection is the norm. But the passion overwhelms the difficulties.

Every time I attend a concert, I am stunned by the adulation the crowd showers upon the performer. I recently saw the Eagles perform. Though they are well beyond their prime and haven't had a hit in recent years, you would never have known it from the decibel level emanating from the crowd. This band was passionate about their music and enjoying every minute of performing it. But even if they weren't very good at making music, they probably still would be jamming out in one of the band member's garages at night and working other jobs during the day.

It's easy to identify those who have found their passions. They're the ones who continue to work whether they are achieving wealth or not. They do what they do because they love it and don't want to give it up.

Michael Jordan discovered this the first time he retired. He didn't need more money and was getting old for his sport. After a few months in retirement, however, Jordan realized that basketball was a part of his life he didn't want to relinquish. The reason he came out of retirement wasn't money. It was passion. The intersection of what he did well and what he wanted to do was basketball. This platform allowed him to be very successful and become very wealthy.

Executives who run companies that embody their favorite extra-curricular activities often have identified a platform that encompasses their passion. Most of us are envious of them. They do what they love and make money from it. Bob Puccini, President of MizunoUSA, one of the leading manufacturers of golf clubs and other sporting equipment, is an avid golfer. He chose and stuck with a platform that embodied his passion and has been very successful. I contend that a lot of that success has come because he likes what he does.

Similarly, Ned Post, a 1974 Harvard Business School graduate and the president of Smith Sports Optics (makers of Smith ski goggles) is living in the skiing paradise of Ketchum, Idaho. Rather than toiling on Wall Street or for a consulting firm, he chose an industry that allowed him to indulge his passion for skiing. Many of us don't even consider whether we love our work. We just keep on plugging.

Most people who work for a not-for-profit organization also are merging an outside interest with what they do for a living. They feel a strong connection with the mission of the organization. Often the money is much less important to them than the impact that they are making on the world. The psychic rewards more than make up for any salary differential. I recently had the opportunity to have dinner with Iris Chen, CEO of the "I Have a Dream" Foundations. My discussion with her made me understand the difference between a career that is passion- or mission-related and one that is not.

Iris has the ability and background to do just about anything in business. With a BA from Yale University and a JD/MBA from Harvard, Iris's academic credentials are more than impressive. As would be expected of someone with her pedigree, Iris worked at elite firms such as Sullivan & Cromwell and McKinsey & Company. What I found unexpected was that Iris left McKinsey to join Teach for America in 2003 just as her career was skyrocketing, at least from a financial perspective.

I was dumbfounded. I had never before met someone who had all the qualifications to hit the big time but passed it up. In my world at the time, career success equaled money. The purpose of a person's job was to maximize his or her income. Period. But not for Iris.

When I sat down to dinner with Iris, I found her to be one of the smartest and most insightful women I have ever met. She knows exactly what she wants to do, and she's doing it. Could she be making more money by working for any number of well-known consulting or law firms? Of course. However, Iris has chosen to follow her passion. She does well financially, but more importantly, she loves her job and career choice.

I compare Iris to my ex-husband. While Richard has indeed done very well financially, he has now confided to his children that working for the almighty dollar was pure hell. He was miserable for a long period of time because he was not following his passion; he was chasing the money. Iris has made me rethink the intricacies of career choice. Perhaps our jobs are not all about financial compensation. Perhaps we can break through the stereotypes (and realities) of work's being a grind. Perhaps we really *can* like what we do.

- **Define your audience**

It is impossible to communicate your brand effectively if you don't define and understand your audience first. Just turn on your TV and you will see how well organizations target distinct audiences. If I am watching professional football, I see ads for pickup trucks and Viagra. Companies that sell feminine products are more likely to advertise on Lifetime. Daytime television usually features ads for home cleaning products that are targeted to housewives.

Each company has spent millions of dollars in research to understand which audience is watching which programs. While none of us has that much money to spend researching our audience, each of us can segment our "customers" by deciding who should be the focus of our efforts to communicate our brand.

Who your audience should be depends on who is buying what you have to sell. For example, an entrepreneur will have a different group of people she wants to reach than someone who is more comfortable working for a larger company. If you're looking for a job, think about which companies/industries make sense for you to target based on your preferences. If you're selling yourself internally for promotion or externally for business development, think about the people you are trying to reach. To be most effective, you must understand your audience and then craft appropriate messages for that audience.

If I am just coming out of school and live, eat, and breathe the stock market, then investment banks are my audience for interviews. If I love the advertising world, then I'd better try to impress Madison Avenue. Entrepreneurs follow a different route, one that includes getting in front of private equity investors—or even relatives with cash. Some of these audiences are unique and others overlap. The trick is to be precise and deliberate in defining the right one for you to focus on.

Suze Orman, personal finance author, certified financial planner, and media personality, has done an excellent job of defining her audience. There are many public accounts of her life and career. Born June 5, 1951, in Illinois, Orman's youth did not necessarily point to a career as a business guru. When she was one credit shy of receiving her degree, Orman packed a bag, moved to Berkeley with some friends, and became a waitress at the Buttercup Bakery, during which time she completed her degree by taking a Spanish class at Hayward State University.

While at the bakery, she secretly wanted to open her own restaurant. When a customer lent Orman money to help her start her dream business, she was on her way. Unfortunately, as fate would have it, Orman invested the money with Merrill Lynch and within three months lost all her assets in a falling market. She was once again broke and knew she couldn't possibly pay off the loan on her bakery job salary.

Orman decided to try her hand at being a stock broker and applied for a position at Merrill Lynch. Although the firm was reluctant to hire her, she got the job and began studying finance. She eventually sued Merrill Lynch for the lost $50,000 and despite the suit continued to work for them becoming a successful stock broker.

She left the firm in 1983 and took a position at Prudential Bache Securities as vice president of investments. Four years later, Orman went out on her own starting the Suze Orman Financial Group. Her main focus has been on helping people who don't want to live paycheck to paycheck—those who want to attain financial freedom. Orman's customers are not financially savvy or wealthy. They are drawn to her knowledge and charisma, both of which set her apart from her competition. Her books, including *The 9 Steps to Financial Freedom*, *The Courage to Be Rich*, and *The Road to Wealth,* and her speaking engagements are targeted to this specific audience—those who don't understand finances well, but who are motivated to learn. That audience is mostly women.

While Orman plays to one specific customer segment, I often have found that I need to pitch different aspects of what I do to different audiences. Depending on what I am trying to achieve, I may look to different groups with very different preferences. For example, if I am trying to sell strategy consulting, I want my customer to be the CEO of the company. His or her job description should read "Chief Strategist" and I want to be that person's right hand.

If I am selling operational consulting, my customer is quite different. I may target the VP of Supply Chain if I can help the company lower its procurement costs or the VP of Corporate Development if I'm selling merger integration. My customer can change depending on the situation, and I have to be flexible enough to know how to most effectively interact with each one.

- **Refine your message**

Once you get comfortable with the fact that you are a brand and have identified your passion and audience, you will want to turn your focus to communication. I try to make sure that my message to my customer is consistent, unique, and succinct. I look for differentiators that distinguish me in the market and make people remember me. I also make sure that my brand will resonate with my audience.

There are many people who have conveyed their brand so effectively to their audiences that they end up defining a genre. A good example of this is Martha Stewart, founder of Martha Stewart Omnimedia. Because she was so effective in focusing and communicating her brand, Stewart was able to serve a prison sentence and barely miss a beat. Prior to her legal problems in 2004, she gained success through a variety of business ventures including publishing, broadcasting, and merchandising.

In 1976, after a career as a model and a stockbroker, Stewart began a catering business; over time, she built it into a multimillion dollar company that made her a billionaire on paper when it went public in 1999. In the May 1995 issue, *New York* magazine declared her "the definitive woman of our times." In 2001, she was named the third most powerful woman in America by the *Ladies' Home Journal.*

The secret to Martha Stewart's success was—and still is— effective messaging about her personal brand: home-made meals and decorations; hearth and home; pretty packages; and do-it-yourself charm. Martha communicated to her audience that if they followed "her" way, their lives would be richer, fuller, and more fulfilling. This message was clear and focused. Many people bought it and are still buying it. The fact that this type of work was clearly her passion made her even more successful. The product of a father who was a talented handyman and a mother who was a gifted homemaker, Stewart knew how to sell what she had learned.

Following her release from prison in 2005, Stewart launched a highly publicized comeback, returned to daytime television, and rebuilt her reputation. If she had not been so effective in communicating and solidifying her brand over many years in the marketplace, her return to success would have been much more difficult, if not impossible.

Suze Orman, who is very accomplished at defining her audience, is also good at focusing and refining her message. She lets her customers know that she is *the* source to get them on their road to financial freedom and wealth. Since she's female, she is sending a message specifically to women: they can be like her and succeed. Her message is, "Follow me. I will show you the way to financial freedom and a debt-free life."

While it may feel awkward to consider yourself as a brand, it can help you be objective about yourself and your career preferences and prospects. Create a personal elevator speech— a sound bite of a minute or less that describes you and your career; you should be able to deliver it in the time it takes to ride a few floors on an elevator. If you are clear about how you see yourself, what you do best, and what feeds your passions, others will know you better and remember you at opportune times.

If you treat yourself the same way you would a product or service marketed by your company, you will allocate your time more effectively and receive a better payback from your efforts.

Quick Tips

The quiz below can help you identify your passions and understand whether or not you have branded yourself. Some of the questions are multiple choice, some open-ended. Answer them truthfully and you will begin to learn how clear you are about what you really want.

1. My current job makes me feel (circle all that apply)

    a. Excited

    b. Exhausted

    c. Stressed out

    d. Energized

    e. Valuable

    f. Like a cog in a wheel

    g. As if I'm in the right place

    h. As if I'd rather be *anywhere* else

2. Risk is something:

    a. I'm willing to take

    b. I'm afraid of and won't take

    c. I'm afraid of but willing to take

3. I am happiest when:

    a. Working with a lot of people

    b. Working in small groups

    c. Working alone

4. What I like best about my current job is _____.

5. What I like least about my current job is _____.

6. The 3 things I do best are:

    a._____

    b._____

    c._____

7. The way others see me is consistent with how I see myself. True / False

8. My personal elevator speech is:

    a. Too short

    b. Too long

    c. Just right

    d. Non-existent

    e. What's an elevator speech?

9. My networking activities are focused on specific individuals or groups.

    True / False

10. If I won the lottery, I would (circle all that apply):

    a. Stay in my current job

    b. Run for the elevator and find something I really want to do

    c. Buy the company and fire my boss

Chapter Nine:
LUCKY SEVEN RULE 5: OWN THE ILLUSION OF CONFIDENCE

"If I have lost confidence in myself, I have the universe against me." – Ralph Waldo Emerson

When tennis great Roger Federer struts onto center court, he exudes confidence. His opponents fear him before the first ball is struck. Those who follow or play sports know that less than 30 percent of winning is about athletic ability. The rest is what Donna Lopiano calls "the illusion of confidence."

Extraordinary men and women cloak themselves in this illusion of confidence. By this I mean that even if they aren't feeling inwardly confident or aren't actually sure that they can do the job, they don't let the outside world know. Fear of failure is rare among successful business*people* in general and especially among successful business*men*.

In his book *What Got You Here Won't Get You There*, Marshall Goldsmith observes, "All of us in the workplace delude ourselves about our achievements, our status, and our contributions." He continues to tell us how "we

- Overestimate our contributions to a project.
- Take credit, partial or complete, for successes that truly belong to others.
- Have an elevated opinion of our professional skills and our standing among our peers.
- Exaggerate our projects' impact on net profits because we discount the real and hidden costs built into them ... ."

This description does not fit many women I know but it sure describes successful men. Goldsmith calls these characteristics "delusions of success." I call them illusions of confidence. Successful people and especially men always believe they have the capability within themselves to make positive things happen.

My former husband, Richard, is a great example of a person who portrays confidence even though he may not always feel it. Although now retired with plenty of money, he was flying helicopters around San Francisco Bay and earning $200 a week when I first met him. We once had to dump change out of our college beer steins in order to scrounge up enough money to go out for a drink on a Saturday night.

When I moved to Boston to attend business school, Richard was still flying helicopters in the Bay Area but desperate to find a job on the East Coast. The cross-country commute wasn't cutting it. Luckily, through family connections, he was able to land employment in Boston in the investment banking industry—his first "real" job.

He was 29 years old and knew nothing about investment banking. Due to his age, he was hired as an assistant vice president. This meant that his peers and, worse, his subordinates knew a lot more about how to do the job than he did. However, because of his position, they assumed he knew more than they.

Richard didn't let them in on his secret nor did he let them down. He confidently went in to work each day as though he knew what he was doing and scurried home each night to study up on the subject. He now admits that he often didn't feel the confidence he exuded in the workplace. He even admits to a couple of sleepless nights. However, he always delivered more than was expected.

Within a couple of months, he was hired away to work at a much more prestigious firm in an area that, of course, he knew nothing about. He continued to march forward—confidently.

I know that playing sports at an elite level taught me to demonstrate a level of self-assurance on the court that I wasn't always feeling, and I believe that I have transferred at least some of that self-assurance to the workplace. I usually feel comfortable enough in my abilities to jump in with both feet and hope for the best. At Salomon Brothers (the "bite the ass off a bear" investment bank), the results were beyond my wildest dreams.

I joined Salomon Brothers in 1984 as an associate in Corporate Finance. What an elite group we thought we were—the supposed cream of the crop from the best business schools in the country. I was living large in Manhattan, making more money than I needed or deserved. I thought I would never leave.

Then I learned about a position where I could run an entire region for fixed income derivatives. Derivatives? What the heck were derivatives? I knew nothing about puts, calls, caps, swaps, strips, and straddles. They sounded like plays in some bizarre game, but they meant big money and were among the sexiest instruments in the financial world at that time.

At the ripe old age of 28 and armed with a boatload of confidence but not much else, I left Manhattan for Atlanta. Within a year, I had taken my office from last to first place in the country for sales of fixed income derivatives, was again making more money than I thought possible, and having the time of my life.

Unfortunately, I know many more men than women who are comfortable accepting a position or promotion for which they feel they might not be qualified. The results of a recent McKinsey & Company study show that though female employees are eight percent more likely than men to meet performance expectations, they are less likely to apply for promotions. Many women are afraid to accept unfamiliar opportunities and the inherent risks they bring.

Even though we are the newcomers on the block in the marketplace, we do not have to be less confident. Sometimes when you're on the outside looking in or below looking up, everything seems larger than life and scary. But it's not nearly as intimidating when you're on the inside, says Lacey Lewis, the senior vice president of Mergers & Acquisitions at Cox Enterprises. I agree with Lacey.

Appearing more confident than you may feel is not difficult. From observation and personal experience, I advocate the following:

- **Hold your fear in check and take the chance**

There's a book called *Feel the Fear and Do It Anyway.* That's good advice. The world is filled with people who take a chance and reach improbable levels of success, even as they feel that prickly edge of fear. They question whether they can really do it. They wonder if they will be labeled a fraud or an imposter, although imposter syndrome strikes women far more often than men. My ex-husband surely felt some fear as he started new jobs, but under-performance was not a top-of mind concern. There are more than a few politicians who go for the brass ring and get it before worrying about exactly what to do with it.

My favorite example is Arnold Schwarzenegger: Mr. Universe turned movie star turned politician. His good looks and athletic ability caused Schwarzenegger to be recognized worldwide as a famous bodybuilder and Hollywood action hero. A generous dose of confidence and the fearlessness to pursue his dreams are the qualities that enable him to enjoy his current status as a successful businessman and California's 38th governor.

Schwarzenegger was born in Austria in 1947 and at 20 became the youngest person ever to win the Mr. Universe title. He came to America shortly thereafter, winning an unprecedented 12 more world bodybuilding titles. He emigrated to the U.S. determined to live the American dream, earned a college degree from the University of Wisconsin and became a U.S. citizen in 1983. Three years later he married broadcast journalist Maria Shriver.

At this point, he was already showing a great deal of confidence by marrying into one of the most prominent and wealthiest families in the country. But he wasn't finished. He outdid himself by running for governor of California and winning. There were no characteristics that this body builder and action hero had that qualified him to hold this political position other than intelligence and confidence. I have no doubt that he felt some fear in being charged to run the country's largest and arguably most diverse state—and one that in and of itself is one of the largest economies in the world. He summoned the courage and confidence to follow his dream and take the office.

- **Use what you know**

If you are in a situation where almost everything is new, focus on anything that's familiar to you. There always will be some aspect of your new company, job, or role that overlaps with your previous experience and knowledge.

Once in office, Schwarzenegger was quick to use his understanding of self-branding and sports to his advantage and gained immediate credibility. In his prior careers, he had been very successful at promoting himself, and he put that skill to use. He has been California's most effective marketing tool, traveling across the country and around the world extolling California-grown products, cutting-edge technologies, and the state's diverse travel destinations. He also has used his knowledge of sports and background as an internationally recognized athlete to restore health and fitness as a top priority in his state.

When I am in a new situation, it always surprises me to find that while I may not know as much as others in a particular area, I also know a lot about things they don't. I joined one consulting firm that focused primarily on operations, while my background was in strategy. At first I wasn't as comfortable as I had been at my previous strategy firms, but I quickly focused on what I knew and how it meshed with what the group was delivering.

Every project has a strategy component that sets up what needs to be done operationally. Voilà! I found my niche—playing the role of strategy subject matter expert for my office and strategic advisor to performance improvement projects. I was able to impart my knowledge to others by teaching them the finer aspects of strategy consulting. I wrote white papers and held "lunch and learns" for the office. I used what I knew to maintain my confidence level.

- **Practice the look of confidence**

The next time you are at a networking or social function, observe people as they come into the room. Some enter as if they own the place, others as if they're afraid of the crowd. The rules of confidence dictate that you must have the look of ownership.

Because of my sports background, I have an athletic stance and walk. My shoulders are back and my head is high. I am told that this helps me appear confident. I never worry about encountering a room of people I don't know (I figure I'll find at least one decent soul to talk to) or attending a meeting with high-level executives, who are, in reality, only people. I advocate tackling these situations boldly; walk in with your gaze forward and posture erect. You are ready to conquer the world!

To perfect "the look," you will need to master good eye contact. Eye contact is a non-verbal dominance cue. When they are speaking, those with higher status in the workplace maintain eye contact with lower-status individuals. Conversely, low-status individuals tend not to maintain eye contact regardless of whether they are speaking or being spoken to.

Therefore, maintaining eye contact is critical to portraying confidence. When you are speaking to one person, focus your attention on him or her rather than letting your eyes roam around the room—wandering eyes convey nervousness, discomfort, or lack of interest in the person in front of you. That's insulting. If you are interacting with a group, be sure that you make eye contact with each one of them. You will appear more confident if you bring everyone into your circle.

One note of caution, however. Eye contact that's too intense can be unnerving to others, as it can be interpreted as sexual invitation or conversely, an attempt to intimidate. You want to show interest, not frighten people to death. Like appropriate dress, appropriate eye contact is what you want to achieve.

Choose what you wear carefully. You can be too formal or too casual, depending on the situation. When we have "jeans Friday" in my office, I wear jeans. When I am meeting with a banker or lawyer whose office mandates business dress, I wear a suit or its equivalent. It's true that women have more license than men regarding what is acceptable workplace attire. For example, women can wear dressy separates when an occasion requires formal business dress, while men can't even get away with a blazer and slacks. The key is to be appropriate. You don't have to look like a man but you don't want look out of place.

Barack Obama has perfected the look of confidence in stature, body language, and dress. His head is always high, he often has a broad smile on his face, and he always appears self-assured. When he walks into a room, he makes people turn their heads, not just because of his position, but because of the charisma he exudes. When giving a speech, he seems to look at each person in the audience individually. I remember when he was first elected to the United States Senate years ago and I saw him on TV. I knew then that this was a man who was going places. Obama makes those around him feel as if he is always in control.

The way you look is not the only way you can convey confidence. Certain speech styles also are associated with power and confidence. Language can move you through the business hierarchy or keep you frozen in your current position. In their book, *Power in Language: Verbal Communication and Social Influence,* Sik Hung Ng and James J. Bradac state that, "both male and female communicators receive higher ratings of competence, status, dynamism, and attractiveness when they use a high power style [of speaking]." While I recommend picking up their book or another dedicated to communication, here's some food for thought. To see if your speech is leading toward or away from power, ask yourself the following questions:

- Do my statements often sound like questions?
- Do I hedge my opinions with phrases such as, "This may sound crazy, but ..." or "I may be wrong but ..."?
- Do I apologize for my viewpoints?
- Do I use tags at the end of my statements (*e.g.*, "We are going to present our analysis tomorrow, OK?")?
- Do I hesitate before giving opinions?

If your answer to any of these questions is "yes," your speech probably is perceived by both your male and female colleagues as weak. Focus on being direct, clear, and confident in your speech and you will be perceived as a stronger businessperson.

- **Know how to pick up the pieces of failure**

It's inevitable that we will fail at some point in our lives. I waltzed through most of my years feeling that I was immune to failure. Then, when I was in my mid-forties, I got divorced. On top of this spectacular failure, I experienced a few more in quick succession. I was ill-equipped to handle the fall-out. Nobody had given me the instruction manual on how to pick up the pieces and move on. But if you're going to have the confidence to take a chance, you have to know what to do if you fall on your face—or any other part of your anatomy.

When failure seems inevitable, you have a couple of choices: stick it out and try to salvage what you can, or move on. In both scenarios, I have found it best to admit your mistakes; most people are more forgiving than you think. Examples abound of those who have stuck it out and those who have not. There is no right answer.

When I was working for Salomon Brothers in the mid-1980s, interest rate swaps were a hot new instrument and Salomon was one of the top firms selling them. We had a very experienced "swaps" team that was coveted by other Wall Street firms.

I was able to observe our team first hand. There were indeed superstars who knew their stuff. There were also junior salesmen who relied on the knowledge of the senior team members and Salomon's pricing technology. These younger salesmen were in their early twenties, yet they made hundreds of thousands of dollars a year. Pretty heady stuff for these young turks. They became cocky very quickly.

One in particular had had an outstanding year and was therefore very marketable. Another investment bank that was just building its swap desk wooed him away for a hefty sum. He was excited about his new job and especially about the money he would make. Until he got there.

He quickly realized that this bank didn't have the software or knowledge to price swaps; they assumed he was bringing this ability with him. Unfortunately, he had relied one hundred percent on Salomon's pricing system and the expertise of the senior sales staff. He even called his previous colleagues asking how he could access the software from his new firm. Not possible. He was soon exposed for not having the knowledge he was paid to have.

There was a lot of money involved and though he was unable to deliver the goods, the company kept him on. He used his inherent self-confidence to convince the firm he was still an asset to them: They needed his sales abilities and he would make them a lot of money. He took the failure in stride, admitted his shortcomings, and in the end still won the game.

Quick Tip
Practice "walking on water" daily

Our assignment as women is to use the illusion of confidence to ensure our career progress. In business as in sports, if you believe in yourself enough and portray confidence, others will naturally believe in you, too. Women everywhere can learn from those who are ultra-confident. Rather than worrying about whether or not we can do a job, we should focus on getting the position and then delivering the goods.

When I was applying to business schools, a savvy friend told me that my essays had to portray a "masculine" amount of confidence. She said I had to make people think I walked on water daily, as if water-walking were the most natural thing in the world. That's what I challenge you to do now. If we start with the walk-on-water daily mindset, we may begin to get to the same level of confidence as our male counterparts.

Chapter Ten:
LUCKY SEVEN RULE 6:
REACH BEYOND YOUR
COMFORT ZONE

"Familiarity is a magician that is cruel to beauty but kind to ugliness." – Marie Louise de la Ramee

We are all comfortable with what is familiar to us, and we want to wrap ourselves in this familiarity like a soft old bathrobe. However, there are times when it's necessary to put on a different outfit and leave the house.

Most of us are products of a rigid educational system that does not encourage individuality. From my earliest years in school, I remember much more emphasis being placed on memorization than on creative thought. We were taught to study for the test rather than to learn something new. I, rightly or wrongly, focused on the end result: grades. My motivation was not in learning *per se* but rather in getting the best marks. It wasn't until I went to business school that I discovered that creative thought—rather than "the one right answer"—would be rewarded.

In the workplace, there are no study questions or Cliff notes. The most important trait for a businessperson in today's economy is having the confidence to go beyond his or her comfort zone and to think in new and inventive ways. Existing products and services may sustain a business for the moment, but novel ideas keep the company growing. If a business isn't innovating, it's dying, so every company is looking for creativity.

When I talk about ability to think differently, I am not implying that you have to be Bill Gates. Creativity can come in the form of everyday inspirations that improve business in some fashion. Creative thought can lead to a new process, a new product, a new service, or an entirely new business.

Nonetheless, creativity can be scary. Innovative thinking means that you break away from the herd. You do things differently from your coworkers. Here are a couple of ways you can assert your creativity and individuality:

- **Expand the definition of your job**

Don't be hemmed in by your position description. Look at the needs of the company as a whole and decide what is within your power or ability to improve. While it may mean reaching beyond your comfort zone now, it also can ensure long-term job security.

My knowledge management team at Andersen Consulting personified the notion of going above and beyond a job description. Officially, each knowledge manager's responsibilities were limited to posting documents for his or her specific industry group on an electronic library and helping the consultants retrieve them.

Unofficially, however, each one became the Central Intelligence Agency for the line consultants. Knowledge managers knew more about what was going on across their areas nationwide than anyone else in the company. They kept up with trends, competitors, and market intelligence. They knew who was new to the company and who had resigned even before most of the partners.

Because I had been a line consultant before I took the position as director of knowledge management, I understood the requirements of a consultant's job inside and out. Consultants were on the road constantly and barely had time to keep up with information related to their clients, let alone stay current with their focus industries, functional areas, office affairs, and personnel issues. They needed go-to people in the back office doing all of these things for them. They needed my knowledge managers.

I therefore coached these managers in a "day in the life of a consultant." They learned to anticipate the consultants' needs. Because they already were well-versed in research methods, they were able to stay on top of key trends that were crucial to their respective areas, and because they were physically in the office, they knew everything going on there as well. They became a treasure trove of information for those lacking the time or proximity to get these data themselves.

Having knowledge made them valuable; being hyper-responsive to the consultants' requests made them indispensible. Because they expanded their roles beyond what was expected of them, these knowledge managers didn't have to worry much about being replaced.

Most top-level executives, both men and women, have gone beyond their job descriptions to get where they are. They see an opportunity to add value to their company and capitalize on it. I am always impressed by the analyst who not only gets me the information I asked for in a timely fashion but who also gets me more than I was looking for and answers questions I hadn't thought of.

Some people are so creative that they expand or create not just a job but rather an entire industry. Imagine the creativity—and guts—it took for Fred Smith to envision and found FedEx. According to the Academy of Achievement's biography, Smith had an early vision for starting the company. While attending Yale University, Smith wrote a paper on the need for reliable overnight delivery in a computerized information age. His professor did not agree with the premise and Smith's recollection is that he received a low grade for this effort. It's surprising that he didn't give up on his idea then and there.

After graduation, Smith enlisted in the Marine Corps and served two tours of duty in Vietnam. While in the military, he observed military procurement and delivery procedures carefully and continued to harbor his dream of creating a worldwide network to provide overnight commercial delivery. In 1971, after he left the Service, Smith raised $80 million and launched

Federal Express. "I wanted to do something productive after blowing so many things up," he later told an interviewer.

The delivery service began by handling small packages and documents with fourteen jets. In the first two years, the venture lost $27 million and was on the verge of bankruptcy. At one point in order to make payroll, he raided the family trust fund without his sisters' permission—they later sued him.

In spite of losing his investors' money, he was able to negotiate creatively with his banks and keep the company afloat. In an NBC interview he recounted, "I was in Chicago when I was turned down for the umpteenth time from a source I was sure would come through. I went to the airport to go back to Memphis and saw on the TWA schedule a flight to Las Vegas. I won $27,000 starting with just a couple of hundred and sent it back to Memphis. The $27,000 wasn't decisive, but it was an omen that things would get better."

Smith was able to envision an entire industry that others, including his Yale professor, scoffed at. He persevered and won. Along the way, his creativity and ability to think of new ways to get the job done served him well.

- **Know when the safe route is the wrong route**

Moving beyond your comfort zone also can mean agreeing to do something that is unfamiliar—and perhaps frightening. I'm sure that Fred Smith had a few sleepless nights back in the early '70s, but I'm also sure he's sleeping well now.

I am a risk-averse person, but I know when the safe route is the wrong route. I am willing to take a calculated risk when the expected reward is big enough.

I recently had the opportunity to leave the comfort and stability of a large firm and join another that was in start-up mode. This was a difficult decision for me. I would be giving up a large base salary and ease of entry to prospective clients, but I also would say goodbye to the frustrating bureaucracy and loss of control that came with working for a large company. I would gain involvement in the leadership of the new venture, reap potentially greater financial rewards, and contend with less political maneuvering, but I also would lose all the security that comes with working for a well-known firm.

As I pondered my decision, I realized that I would be giving up something else as well: status. I always had worked for companies that weren't just big names; they were the elite of the elite. Salomon Brothers and Goldman Sachs, two of my former employers, were so-called "bulge bracket" investment banks in the '80s and '90s. Getting a job at one of these firms was considered a coup. When I first worked for Bain & Company in the 1984, all of the consultants had MBAs—and not just any MBAs; their degrees were from Harvard, Stanford, or Wharton. Bain was then and still is considered one of the top three strategy consulting firms in the world.

If I joined this fledgling firm I would be giving up the social and business recognition I had enjoyed due to the names of my employers. I had to confront the fact that my ego might be one of the factors keeping me from taking a chance My worst fear might be realized; I might fail. What to do?

I decided that the safe route was the wrong route for me and joined the start-up. I quickly realized that I am by nature very entrepreneurial and that large companies tend to stifle my performance. I reveled in the start-up atmosphere. The psychic income I gained from helping this new company flourish more than made up for my worries about financial stability and status. Because I was doing what I liked, the money soon followed.

I have a good friend who found himself at a similar crossroads. Very intelligent and with an MBA from a top school, he had worked for a commercial bank for more than 20 years. In 2007, as the banking industry began a serious downturn due mainly to poor investing in sub-prime mortgages, he took a closer look at the company and industry in which he worked. He was no longer happy with what he saw.

In mid-2008, a fast-paced money management firm knocked on his door asking him to leave the bank and work for them. His decision was very similar to the one I had faced both in what he would be giving up and what he would be getting. His personality is even more risk averse than mine, which made leaving the familiar even more difficult for him.

After much negotiation and thought, he left the security of the bank for the excitement and opportunity of the investment management firm. After leaving, he wondered why he had stayed with his previous company so long. He thrived in the new environment He has not looked back.

Meg Whitman, the former CEO of eBay also left a safe environment for a far riskier one—and won. Whitman graduated from Harvard Business School in 1979 and immediately packed her bags for California to work for Bain & Company. After Bain, she took a number of high-level positions at well-known, large corporations including Disney, Stride Rite and FTD, in highly visible global positions. Many would say that at this point in her career Whitman had made it.

She had something different in mind. In 1988, a man named Pierre Omidyar came to Whitman and asked her to run his small startup: an auction site called eBay, which at the time was little more than an online flea market with only 30 employees and $4 million in revenues. Impressed by eBay's growing community of users and intrigued by the Internet's opportunities, Whitman reached way beyond her comfort zone and accepted his invitation. She is now credited with beating back competitors, charlatans, and skeptics and keeping eBay firmly ensconced as the pre-eminent online auction site.

When Whitman stepped down from her position as CEO in 2007, eBay boasted 15,000 employees and more than $6 billion in revenue. With an estimated personal net worth of more than $1 billion, Whitman is now on the list of the wealthiest women in business—all because she refused to play it safe.

Greg Owens, the partner I worked with at Andersen Consulting, took what many thought was a chance in 1999 by leaving the comfortable, sure income of Andersen to become CEO of Manugistics, a supply-chain software company. "I have the opportunity to be at the helm of a turnaround situation," he told me. "If it flies, my upside is almost limitless. If it fails, I'll still be relatively young and I'll have on my résumé that not only was I a partner at Andersen, but I also was CEO of a decent-sized company. I'll still be extremely marketable."

It is difficult to argue with that logic—especially since Greg became a multimillionaire when he sold his appreciated stock a few years later. Taking a calculated risk that brings you out of your fuzzy bathrobe and puts you into a new suit can provide a big payback.

I have often wondered if women in the workplace are actually more creative than men. It is not that women are born more creative, but rather that we have had to hone this skill to open up opportunities for ourselves in a male-dominated environment. As Lacey Lewis of Cox Enterprises observes, "You have to be just that much better than your male counterparts." Because of this, women should be even better equipped to increase our role definitions and reach for more than what is expected of us.

We should also want to expand our horizons for reasons other than succeeding in our current companies or jobs. The more we learn and experience, the more marketable we are for other positions and organizations. The next time you draft your personal development plan, be sure to include opportunities that make you stretch your mind and help you pave your way to your new future.

Quick Tips

See how willing you are to push beyond what's comfortable and familiar by honestly answering the following questions:

1. I ask for new assignments that challenge me.
   a. Often
   b. Sometimes
   c. Rarely
   d. Never

2. I go above and beyond what is expected of me.
   a. Often
   b. Sometimes
   c. Rarely
   d. Never

3. I look for new learning opportunities
   a. Often
   b. Sometimes
   c. Rarely
   d. Never

4. I am willing to take a calculated risk even if I am not certain of the outcome.
   a. Often
   b. Sometimes
   c. Rarely
   d. Never

5. I do not stay with my current employer because of job security; I like what I do. ___Yes ___No

Chapter Eleven:
Lucky Seven Rule 7: It's Not Life or Death. It's Business

"If we couldn't laugh, we would all go insane." – *Jimmy Buffett*

A couple of years ago I was playing golf—poorly. As I got more frustrated with myself and my game, my playing partner looked at me and said, "Erin, don't take yourself so seriously. Nobody else does." She was right. I was indeed putting too much pressure on myself and playing worse because of it. I was acting as though I were competing in a national tournament rather than out for a fun round of eighteen.

In the workplace, I have seen people take themselves far too seriously. Whenever business is down or big money is involved, the workplace hunkers down as if it's under siege by terrorists. But it isn't. No lives are at stake here.

The problem with a disproportionate reaction to business and economic issues is that it increases the anxiety level for everyone involved. When too much weight is placed on matters that are not life or death issues, an inappropriate level of stress is created, and stress affects our performance and health.

As Gretchen Hirsch says in *The Complete Idiot's Guide to Difficult Conversations:*

> The feeling of being in danger unleashes a chain reaction of bodily changes. Adrenaline and other chemicals cascade into the system. The pupils of our eyes dilate so we can see better, even in the dark. Our hearts beat faster to get more blood to the muscles we use to escape or fight. ... The liver converts glycogen into sugar for quick energy. The sweat glands get busy to keep us cool in the heat of battle. Breathing speeds up to oxygenate the blood. The body brings its full wisdom to shield us from danger.

Unfortunately, she continues, our time-pressured, competitive, unpredictable environment "activates our fight or flight mechanism far too often. Our bodies are overloaded with stress chemicals that keep us hyper-alert and on edge." Not surprisingly, that's not good for us. And when we are constantly concerned with survival, our thought processes grind to a halt. We can't make good decisions or, in some cases, any decisions at all.

I have experienced this uber-serious management-by-fear several times in my career, once while working for a hard-driving consulting firm. The economy had taken a big dive, and the consulting industry also was having trouble. Those of us who had been in the business for a while knew this was a cyclical phenomenon and we would survive. Our office managing partner felt differently.

He began scheduling twice-weekly meetings of the leadership team to discuss the situation. He told us that he was putting in 14-hour days and waking up "at least two times a night" due to our office's lack of prospects in the pipeline.

And worse, he told us that he could not shoulder the burden alone. If the members of the leadership team weren't experiencing the same level of insomnia as he, then we were not serious enough about our careers. I believed he was clearly in need of recalibration.

In this case, the top executives were doing everything they could to sell work. The economy was just not cooperating; the old adage about not being able to squeeze water from a stone applied here.

The situation was indeed serious from a business perspective, but it wasn't life-threatening. Rather than improving performance in the office, the managing partner's action ratcheted up the anxiety level and caused some team members to reassess their decisions to join the firm.

When professionals take themselves and their jobs too seriously, they lose perspective. Cancer is serious; business is not. Those who are able to focus on the bottom line without getting too wound up in the drama win.

Often those who enjoy the highest pay are the ones who take themselves the most seriously and lose balance in their lives. The never-ending quest for more money becomes a disease. I have seen colleagues and friends lose sight of the fact that they are allowed to—and should—get enjoyment from their work. Rather than working to live, they become people who live to work.

The reason I left Wall Street was that most investment bankers take themselves ultra-seriously and the atmosphere can become poisonous. But there are always exceptions to the rule. One of the first people I met when I joined Goldman Sachs in 1986 was a man who ran the J. Aaron commodities division. A Brooklyn-born, Harvard-educated son of a postal worker, he was making more money than his parents ever had. Yet he seemed able to take all of the exaggerated wealth in stride. He was humorous and even self-deprecating at times—and he did his job extremely well.

This man is Lloyd Blankfein, now CEO of Goldman and one of the most influential businessmen in the world. Even though he made more than $68 million in 2007, I have no doubt that he is still keeping things in perspective.

When the economic situation worsened in 2008, Blankfein, along with six other top Goldman executives, asked the board's compensation committee to grant them no bonuses, a request that was approved. A public relations ploy perhaps, but compare it to the actions of John Thain, then the CEO of Merrill Lynch, several months later.

For the final quarter of 2007, Merrill posted a net loss of nearly $10 billion—the biggest loss in the company's 94 year history—and wrote down $16.7 billion of troubled assets affected by subprime lending. The stock immediately plummeted more than 10 percent. Merrill predicted this to be the end of the carnage. They were mistaken. By the end of 2008, they had been acquired by Bank of America and posted a new record loss of $15.3 billion for the 2008 fourth quarter.

It was within this context that on December 8, 2008, the *Wall Street Journal* reported that Thain had suggested to his directors that he be awarded a year-end bonus of as much as $10 million. The board understandably resisted. It also became public knowledge that upon joining the firm a year or so earlier, Thain had hired the same designer to refurbish his office as Barack Obama has hired for the White House. The new look came complete with must-have items such as an $87,000 office rug.

On January 22, 2009, Thain resigned from his post. "His situation was not working," commented a Bank of America spokesman. The different way that Lloyd Blankfein responded to a crisis versus his contemporary John Thain makes a strong statement about each man's values and perception of himself. It's easy to spot the one who has an elevated, intense opinion of his abilities.

In addition to losing perspective in their lives, those who take themselves too seriously run the risk of ruling with their emotions rather than with their intellect. They are less able to take a deep breath and assess a situation rationally.

The managing partner I previously mentioned became very emotional when pushing for everyone to work harder and worry more. He didn't realize that his inability to stay calm when times were tough caused him to appear less professional and actually lowered the productivity of the office.

Most people mistake emotion for passion. While I encourage people to be passionate about their work, I caution them to check their emotions at the door. Many would say that this is impossible. Passion, after all, is a constellation of emotions including enthusiasm, desire, eagerness, and vivacity.

The trick is to be passionate about what you do for a living without unleashing a wide range of emotions on unsuspecting peers, subordinates and/or leaders. It's okay to be avid about your work and the organization's goals, but it's not okay to be emotionally volatile, flying off the handle, berating people, or causing undue tension among your co-workers or subordinates.

Emotional volatility makes problem solving, the very crux of business, more difficult. Intense emotions in the workplace add to the difficulty of doing the job at hand. When co-workers are overly emotional, they stew and worry rather than focus on the tasks that will move the company forward.

I have seen many top executives who took themselves very seriously also internalize their jobs and take them too personally. I once worked with an executive who called meetings to discuss the company's financials whenever the numbers were positive. His presentations always included lots of gesticulation and fanfare. Everyone thought he was great: He was showing passion and generating enthusiasm!

In retrospect, his behavior was a warning sign, an indicator of an oversized and overly sensitive ego. He needed the adulation of his team when he presented the numbers to them as a group.

However, when the news wasn't as rosy, his coworkers soon realized that he was defensive and did not welcome probing questions. The "happy" meetings he called were only exercises in self-aggrandizement and a waste of time for all involved.

Women on the way up experience pressures—real and imagined—that their male colleagues do not. Many of us, as Lacey Lewis of Cox Enterprises mentioned, feel that to succeed we have to be better than the men. I admit to having these thoughts. For example, almost all of my doctors are females. I choose them because I want my doctor to be the most competent and capable practitioners available; I couldn't care less about popularity or who everyone else sees. My rationale for picking women is that I think they have to be that much smarter than the guys to have gotten where they are. Therefore, they are the best.

Many women in the workplace feel the same way about themselves as I do about my doctors ("I have to be smarter, more capable, a better salesperson, a harder worker"). They add pressure to themselves in order to achieve. This pressure leads to undue stress and often takes the fun out of our jobs.

I have a friend who works in marketing for a mid-sized regional accounting firm. She puts in an inordinate number of hours every week, telling me this behavior is necessary to "turn the place around." The problem is that she felt this way when she worked for her previous firm and the firm before that. It's possible that she just happens to accept roles with companies that are hopelessly out of control, but not probable. And I guarantee that her male co-workers are not burning the midnight oil with her. She lets us all know she is usually working alone into the wee hours. She feels she has to work longer hours and produce more than the guys to be a success at her job. In other words, she has to outperform the men.

Women often have the pressure of not knowing what their company or the workplace expects from them. We are told to be assertive but not too assertive. Most industries, companies and organizations reward competitive, aggressive behavior if it comes from a man. As Ann Hopkins of PWC painfully realized, the workplace is less tolerant of typical business behavior from its females. We are expected to somehow balance exhibiting the necessary, masculine traits of business with those that are expected of us as women.

Those of you who have watched the TV show *The Closer* know what I mean. Brenda Johnson, played by Kyra Sedgwick, is a detective who is smart and, of course, always solves the case when the men can't. She is also pretty, petite, and wears a lot of make-up. She doesn't come across as tough and aggressive.

With her Southern drawl and deliberate charm, Johnson lulls her colleagues and the "bad guys" into thinking she's an air-head when in reality, she is the only one who gets to the answer. It possible that the reason this is one of the most popular crime shows on TV is that Johnson is able to maintain the fine balance of being a smart woman without being intimidating to the men.

Women with children often have an even more difficult time managing perceptions. Many experience the "damned if you do, damned if you don't" syndrome. If you take too much time off, you're put on the "mommy track." If you work too much, you're a bad mother.

I recently read an article in *The Week* magazine entitled, "France: A Justice Minister Shuns Maternity" that highlights the difficulty that businesswomen with children face from the standpoint of perception. The article posed the question, "Is France's justice minister a courageous superwoman or bad mother and a disgrace to the feminist cause?" The minister, Rachida Dati, had been called both because she dared to return to work five days after giving birth. Her detractors view her as "a pushy, over-promoted favorite," while her admirers see the incident as an example of "the drive that took this child of Moroccan immigrants to a top government post, one rarely held by women." She is being placed under a microscope that men would never experience.

Most businesswomen with children have the additional responsibility of trying to balance work and family life. This concern is usually not one that troubles their male colleagues. Working two jobs, one with a salary and one paying only psychic income, can be overwhelming and contribute to our putting unintended stress on ourselves. My children, Averil and Pierce, are 18 months apart, and before I packed them off to college, I felt continual pressure to juggle competing interests.

When my children were very young, I agonized over leaving them with a nanny. Would she give them the same amount of attention that I would lavish on them? Would she take them to the park or plunk them in front of a TV despite the house rules against this? Should I get a nanny-cam?

As Averil and Pierce got older, the situation became more difficult rather than easier. Their school celebrated every possible holiday and some I had never heard of—each with its requisite party. And the parents participated. Not wanting my children to feel slighted, I went to the office early and worked late so I could steal away in the middle of the day to play pin the tail on the Halloween pumpkin. My children were also very involved in sports. This meant practices they had to be driven to and games that I had to—and wanted to—attend. I felt as if I were being pulled in 23 different directions.

For me, it all came to a head one night when I was in San Diego on a business trip. We were living in Atlanta, and it was my turn to carpool Averil and a handful of her teammates to their soccer game. Since I was not in town and my husband was—typically—at work, our nanny, Jettie, became the chauffeur.

The gods were clearly not smiling on me that evening: The directions to the location of the game required a Ph.D. to decipher, it was raining hard, and while Jettie was great with the children, she didn't have the best sense of direction even when conditions were perfect. Of course she got lost. This was in the late 1990s when cell phones were not the equivalent of everyone's third arm. She didn't have one.

The phone call from the irate mother of one of the kids in the carpool came not to my husband in Atlanta, but to me. In San Diego. Where was her daughter? What was I going to do about it? And on and on. I called my husband to get him on the case, but without the ability to get in touch with Jettie, there was little that he could do either. We both knew that our nanny was very responsible and would make sure that the children all made it home safely. Trying to convince the mother of this fact was another story.

When my nanny finally deposited the little athletes at the meet, happy and unharmed, the mother was there to greet her daughter. She unleashed a torrent of criticism and abuse on a bewildered and frustrated Jettie, who then called me in San Diego to apologize for the incident. I felt guilty for not being there to drive the carpool myself, and I felt guilty for the abuse to which Jettie had been subjected.

I remember sitting on the bed in my hotel room wondering if it was all worth it. I loved my career and couldn't imagine not working, but the stress of having to deal with both my paying and non-paying jobs was pushing me over the edge. I managed to calm down, extricated my daughter from the carpool (I'd rather pay for a taxi than go through that again), and had a serious talk with my husband about enlisting more help from him.

Due to the stress and pressure that was created from having to balance family and career, I had lost track of what was important to me. I lost joy in my job and joy at home. Once I stepped out of the stress-induced chaos and assessed the situation, what I wanted from life once again came into focus: My family came first and my career second. I was able to logically devise a game plan that worked for me.

Stress increases when workers' work/life values do not match their employers'. I have a friend who cares just as much about sports and staying in shape as he does about his career. Unfortunately, the head of his office does not share this enthusiasm for fitness and believes that time at the gym would be better spent at work. Therefore, my friend regularly sneaks out of the office during the day, unbeknownst to his co-workers, to pursue his passion. Compare the attitude in this office to that of Montgomery Securities in the mid-1980s.

When I was graduating from business school in 1984, those of us who played sports were captivated by San Francisco-based Montgomery Securities. Their management and employees consisted of former nationally ranked and collegiate athletes, tri-athletes, and marathoners. The people at this firm worked hard but found time to pursue their sports passions as well. They understood if you took time in the middle of the day for a quick workout because you could compensate by coming in early and staying late. What mattered was getting the work done, not conforming to a set schedule. Those of us who are able to find an employer who shares our work/life values have an easier time keeping our lives in balance.

I try to keep business in perspective for many reasons, not the least of which is that I have a pair of twenty-something children who view the world as their oyster. They find joy and limitless opportunities in everything they do. One is applying for Fulbright and Truman scholarships and also wants to join Teach for America.

The other has a few entrepreneurial ventures up his sleeve and can't wait to graduate from college so he can get to work. They are naïve, yes, but they are also a breath of fresh air. They help me remember that life can be fun, full of joy in the moment. Ruining present moments with fear and self-absorption isn't good for me or anyone around me. I admit there are still times when my evil "way too serious" alter ego raises its head and I have to stop myself from giving in to its pressure. That is when I repeat my golfing friend's words to myself and laugh.

Quick Tips

Consider taking a personality assessment offered by your company or an executive coach. These tools can help you better understand interpersonal dynamics by looking at behaviors and emotions. They help you perform more effectively in the workplace by making you aware of how you react in different situations and environments.

I recommend the DiSC® profile offered by Inscape Publishing because it is easy to use but rich in theory. It will help you see yourself in a different way and may even get you to lighten up on yourself—and others.

SECTION III:
Score!

Chapter Twelve
WOMEN: THE NEW STYLE OF CORPORATE LEADERSHIP?

"The masculine mystique is founded on the assumption that women can find happiness, self-esteem, and self-fulfillment by emulating and ultimately internalizing the ideology of market-place society; in other words, by becoming the female equivalent of economic, acquisitive man." – Suzanne Gordon, Prisoners of Men's Dreams

Not long ago, a friend of mine told me something that made me both sad and angry. My friend was the president of a small but successful private equity firm, a fund of funds. The company relied heavily on his abilities, but also boasted some young but high-powered talent. He felt that until he could get them up to speed, the success of the firm rested solely in his hands. And now he was on the horns of a dilemma.

His daughter, a top swimmer in the state, was scheduled to compete in the season's culminating meet; the date had been on the calendar for months. It was extremely important to her that both of her parents be present. At this point in his daughter's young life, the meet ranked up there with graduation, marriage, and probably even childbirth.

As fate would have it, a client of my friend's firm had called a couple of days earlier requesting a meeting—on the same day as the swim meet and in another city. This was not a new occurrence. This client often asked the management of the firm to jump, usually at the last minute. Obviously, my friend was torn; there was no way he could be in both places on that day.

His decision process was difficult. On the one hand, his daughter's happiness was very important to him, and he knew it would be devastating to her if he missed her event.

On the other hand, his reputation in the workplace was important to him as well—perhaps more important to him than anything else. He was continually concerned about others' perception of him and his professionalism. He always felt that he had to accommodate his clients' slightest whims without examining alternatives. He feared losing business unless he was available 24/7. This behavior had been a hallmark of his career. His sense of self-importance was greater than his actual importance to the client.

Instead of assuming that his clients and colleagues were human beings and would understand if there was one day when he could not be there in person, he assumed that it was all or nothing. He had to be there *on that day* or make up a lie to cover his absence. He opted to lie, telling everyone that he had missed his flight.

The fact that he ended up taking the meeting by conference call, that all went smoothly, and that the client relationship would not have been jeopardized by holding the meeting the next day, is beside the point. What's important is my friend felt that the rules of the game left him no flexibility. He believed he had to present himself to the business world as someone with no interests other than his job. His career came first and there was no second or third place.

He later told me that his choice to lie was necessary because he wanted to show his employees how to behave. In his opinion, he was leading by example. His analysts didn't know he had lied, and he had demonstrated that personal commitments should never come before the company's needs. The members of his firm and the client would see his giving up the swim meet as "taking one for the team." He had not put his child's athletic event ahead of work. Except that he had.

The irony of all of this is that the message being sent to junior executives was not to give 200 percent to the firm. The message they got was that they could step away from their jobs for a while, but they had to cover their tracks. He was teaching his employees that they could attend to their personal lives as long as they were sneaky and dishonest about it.

As I mentioned, I played competitive tennis for many years. It was in my blood and kept me centered. Even when I was working on Wall Street in the mid-1980s, I wasn't about to give it up due to the rigors of my job. And it was rigorous. We often worked into the wee hours and sometimes all night.

As a lowly first-year associate, I was at the bottom of the corporate totem pole and everything flowed down to me and my fellow newbies. In the spectacularly inefficient system of corporate finance, we often hung around a good part of the day only to have a pile of work dumped on our desks in the late afternoon, requiring us to stay far into the evening to get it done.

This posed a dilemma for me and my desire to continue my tennis activities. My only option was to play at 6am—ugh—before work. Or was it? I realized that I could make good use of that dead time in the middle of the day long as nobody found out. I formulated a plan.

Instead of hanging around with my colleagues in the office waiting for the inevitable afternoon work dump, I played tennis. Leaving my suit jacket on the back of the chair in my cubicle so everyone would assume I was just away from my desk, I clandestinely grabbed my gear and headed to TennisPort in Queens. A subway ride and 30 minutes later, I was happily pursuing my athletic passion. As long as I got back by 2 or 3PM, no one was ever the wiser. My secret excursions never affected the quality of my work or my ability to get it finished by the deadline.

The sad reality about my story and that of my friend is the corporate culture did not cause either of us to choose work over the other activity (although that happens often as well), but it caused us to be dishonest. In my friend's case, the condoning of lies was a very strong statement about the firm's culture.

Perhaps my friend is just not self-confident enough to realize that clients are people, too. More likely, he perceives that the rules of business really are this unbending and rigid. With men such as this in positions of power, those with families or concerns outside their jobs will continue to have a tough time in such corporate cultures. Or they will learn to lie.

There are a couple of ways to ensure that you don't experience an adverse culture in your job:

- **Work in an environment that shares your values**

The easiest way to avoid struggling against principles or unwritten rules that don't match what you want from your job is to find a company whose values mirror yours. If you want to work 80 hours a week and devote everything to your career, I can direct you to numerous organizations that fill the bill. If you want work/life balance, there are now companies that allow for that.

One of these forward-looking companies is the Atlanta-based North Highland Company. A gem within the sea of ultra-competitive management consulting firms, North Highland was founded by Dave Peterson on the premise of work/life balance.

As the story goes, fifteen years or so ago, Dave was working for one of the Big Five consulting firms, sitting at an airport gate waiting for his flight to leave so he could get to his client site. During this time, another plane arrived and disgorged a horde of consultants all traveling to Atlanta to visit *their* clients, whose companies were obviously located in Atlanta.

Dave had an epiphany. Why was he jetting to faraway cities and leaving his family when there were just as many clients to serve right there in his home town? He couldn't think of a good answer, so he started his own company, the basic tenets of which were that it would serve only clients within a certain radius of the city and consultants would rarely get on an airplane. Not only would the employees achieve better balance in their lives but they also would know their clients better because they both lived and worked in the same city. They are able to charge their clients lower all-in costs because of the reduced travel expenses. A win-win for everybody.

The concept took off and North Highland has been wildly successful. Since 1992, they have grown to 17 North American offices each serving only clients within a given geographic area, with a global network of Highland Worldwide partners. Ranked among *Inc.* magazine's 500 fastest-growing private companies in the early part of this century, North Highland was honored with *Consulting* magazine's Best Firms to Work For 2008 Award, placing third among the world's leading consulting companies. The competition included 205 firms.

North Highland was the first company for whom I worked where I didn't feel the constant pressure to extend my hours. Most consultants arrive at the client site at 8:30am and leave by 5:30pm—or earlier if one of their children has a school recital or soccer game. While they never compromise the quality of their work, the North Highland consultants do not feel the need to put in "face time." The first time one of my male colleagues told me he coached his daughter's softball team and therefore had to leave the client's site every Wednesday at 4pm, I was shocked. This would never have been considered appropriate at my previous employers. Most of my former colleagues barely had a life outside of work.

At North Highland, the opposite is true. Most of the consultants have serious outside interests. They are devoting time to their families or training for an ironman or learning how to play a musical instrument. Each one has his or her reason for choosing the North Highland environment and its life-friendly culture.

Many firms charge their clients a fixed fee where the number of hours to be worked is built in to the contract. However, consultants at these firms "ghost hours," meaning they work more hours than they bill or are in the contract. To keep the price to the client reasonable, these consultants perform the modern day equivalent of slave labor—with better pay. And in fairness to these firms, most of the type-A employees who work there are just fine with this arrangement. They are working for the best, and the fact that they don't have a life makes them feel powerful and important. However, North Highlanders bill clients for a 40-hour work week and do not "ghost hours."

The North Highland Company opened my eyes and made me realize that we all have a choice in how we want to work and live. As with everything there are trade-offs, but the decision is ultimately yours.

- **Work to change the values within your company**

I'd like to change many of the corporate rules that govern the workplace. Unfortunately, this is not as easy to do as choosing or switching jobs. Grass roots change is difficult. Real change has to come from the top. According to Esther Wachs Book's *Why the Best Man for the Job is a Woman*, "A new breed of leader is emerging, and that breed is female." I agree with this statement but possibly not for the same reasons that Book asserts.

Book argues that female CEOs are a sign of the revolution taking place in traditionally male-dominated corporate cultures. The world of business is changing, Book writes, and it is women who are best suited to meet the challenges of the modern marketplace. One has only to look at the disaster of 2008, when the world experienced the biggest financial meltdown since 1932, to understand that the way we've done business in the past is not the best recipe for a stable economic future. Instead of The Year of the Woman, we may need The Century of the Woman.

In promoting her view that women can change corporate culture, Book cites seven competencies that she feels are uniquely female and will propel more female CEOs to success:

1. They can sell their visions.
2. They are not afraid to reinvent the rules.

3. They are closely focused on achievement.
4. They show courage under fire.
5. They turn challenges into opportunities.
6. They are aware of customer preferences.
7. They maximize what Book calls "high touch" in an era of high tech.

I find it difficult to believe that these qualities are uniquely female because many successful men also exhibit them. And I disagree that female CEOs are genetically predisposed to be better leaders. However, because it is more difficult for women to climb their way to the top, they develop certain traits for survival and success. Some of these are described in Harvard Business School professor Boris Groysberg's article, "How Star Women Succeed."

Groysberg contends that "unlike men, high-performing women build their success on portable, external relationships—with clients and other outside contacts." Further, "Women considering job changes weigh more factors than men do, especially cultural fit, values, and managerial style." Therefore they are more tuned in to these factors in a company than their male peers.

It stands to reason, then, that women will work to improve the culture and performance of the workplace if we can get to positions of power. The women that Groysberg describes who have made it to the CEO position are already playing a new game and winning. Andrea Jung, CEO of Avon, is one of them.

Jung's life has been a story of success. As reported in Gold-sea.com's article *Executive Sweet,* Jung "was raised for a solid career in a well-paying profession. She was given piano lessons, Mandarin classes and a Princeton education to cultivate her character and refine her cranium." After college, she rose rapidly in the retail industry, first at Bloomingdales, then at I. Magnin and Neiman Marcus, where she became an executive vice president at the age of 32. She subsequently joined Avon and was considered for the CEO position when she was serving as president of Avon Product Marketing Group (U.S.) at age thirty-nine. She actually got the title two years later.

Jung is direct in her style and knows what she wants to accomplish. Upon accepting the CEO position at Avon, she immediately adopted a new vision for the company believing that it could be recognized for more than just selling cosmetics; under Jung's leadership, Avon has become "*The* Company for Women," an organization that enables its sales reps to achieve economic self-sufficiency.

Jung has transformed Avon into a company that improves the lives of women and their families. She has offered loans to sales reps for start-up inventory, made a $450 million investment in breast cancer education and research, and launched a campaign against domestic violence.

By reaching the seat of power and influence, Jung has been able to push forward an agenda that an old-line cosmetics company never would have considered. She says she is driven by a passion to make a difference. Her thoughts about improving the work environment for women? She states, "Women like myself, CEOs, can pave the way for more women to get to the top." Many of us applaud her goal.

The idea of changing corporate culture brings me back to my old mentor, Leslie Christian. While Leslie wasn't the CEO of Salomon, she was the *de facto* head of fixed income derivatives sales. As such, she dictated the culture for the group. Leslie is extremely ethical, logical, and level-headed. Our group operated under those principles.

When I was working for Leslie, I never left my coat on the chair and sneaked off to play tennis. If I had a conflict that took me away from work, I had no problem discussing it with Leslie. She worked to get the job done, not for show. We put in the time necessary and left when we could.

The attitudes of those of us in Leslie's group were different from those of the rest of the firm. While they were worrying about "biting the ass off a bear," we were figuring out how to best serve our clients. Due to the type of person she was, Leslie set a culture that respected the individual while promoting success.

Esther Wachs Book credits women with innately thinking about their inner feelings more than men do, which she believes makes them better leaders. Although I'm not a psychologist, I disagree. I think women listen to and express their feelings because that is what society expects and encourages them to do. We are allowed to be more honest about making our life choices. It's not that men don't want to spend more time with their families or a hobby or a sport, but rather that they feel they aren't allowed to do so. In our society, being a slave to your job means you're a real man.

If I had a dollar for every time I heard men (or women who have learned this trick from men) complain about how much work they have, how much they travel, or how stressed out they are, I'd be rich. They wear their oppression like a badge of honor as they silently bank their high-level salaries. The more they work, the more successful, important, or powerful they feel. Far from being unhappy with the long hours, these workers actually get an ego boost from letting their friends and family know how frazzled and overworked they are. They provide for their families by killing themselves—and they're more than happy to tell you that.

Women are more likely to follow their inner goals than men are. The pressure is off. Society does not expect us to rule the world. But we can. We actually have multiple chances to find out what we like to do, to do it well, and to figure out how it fits into the rest of our lives. As we find our way into the corner offices and executive suites, we also have a chance to change the politics and internal cultures of our companies.

So, ladies, this is your chance. Understand when you have gained enough power and influence to change the rules for your department, division, or maybe the entire company. The time is now. Don't delay. We can and will change the game for future generations, one rule at a time.

2920518

Made in the USA